Patrick Meehan

Innocent Villain

Pan Books London and Sydney

First published 1978 by Pan Books Ltd,
Cavaye Place, London SW10 9PG
© Patrick Meehan 1978
ISBN 0 330 25444 8
Printed and bound in Great Britain by
Hazell Watson & Viney Ltd, Aylesbury, Bucks

Contents

List of illustrations

I would like to place on record my thanks to John Sheard whose editorial advice and assistance was invaluable in the production of this book.

My thanks are also due to George Forbes of the *Glasgow Herald*; and, above all, to Ludovic Kennedy and the members of the Meehan Committee and everyone else who championed my cause.

for my wife Betty,
and for my children, Pat, Sally, Liz and Gary.

1 Innocent villain

It was the irony of the situation that hit me like a hard punch over the heart.

As soon as they shuffled in, all fifteen of them, I knew the impossible was about to happen. It's a cliché in all the crime books, but it is true – juries never look a man in the eye when they are about to pronounce him Guilty. The fifteen men and women who comprised that Scottish jury on Friday October 24th, 1969 looked at their feet, at their bench, at the walls and at the ceiling, everywhere but at me standing in the tiny dock. I wonder if they felt then, just before 5.50 PM, that they were about to make an appalling mistake. I wonder how they feel now, these long years later?

The irony came from the fact that in many ways this was no new situation for me. I have watched many a jury come into court and too often those juries have also looked away. It is one of the crisis times in the life of a professional criminal. Perhaps a surgeon feels the same way when he is about to make the first incision in an operation he knows to be hopeless, or the airline pilot desperately trying to reassure his passengers when he knows the plane is doomed. Long before the foreman stood to announce the verdict, I knew I was doomed: endless spirit-destroying years lay ahead in prison, whose walls and bars and routines I knew all too well. These years, however, would be centuries; the days months; the seconds hours; for this time I was innocent. And this time, the charge was murder.

I doubt whether the ordinary, law-abiding citizen can ever truly understand the working of the criminal mind. I am sure that, to most people, we, the villains, are totally amoral. Because we ignore the law, we ignore all laws, the laws of courtesy, of feelings for our fellow men, the laws of compassion and loyalty, the laws of self respect. The straight citizen cannot believe that we also have our codes, our pride, and our position in a criminal society which has at least as many stratas, as many successes and failures, as ordinary society. We have our hard workers – the

11

'earners' – and we have our layabouts, who prey on the weak and the wretched because that is the easiest way. They are the ones who never succeed in crime, because easy pickings are never big pickings. They are the ones who tend to substitute muscle for skill. They are the ones who hurt innocent people.

I am not proud of my life – I realize now that I have wasted what talents I was given – but I have the underworld's pride of being one of the élite: a 'peterman' – a safe-cracker, a planner and a highly skilled technician; a 'straight' villain who specialized in diverting large sums of money from institutions with a lot of it – like banks and big stores – to others who had little, like me. It is a job which is at least as demanding as anything in ordinary society. More importantly, I have lived my criminal life to a very strict code. I have never entered anyone's home illegally, because going into houses which are likely to be occupied presents risks which I have been unwilling to take. One is the risk of being surprised and identified. Another, far more serious, is the risk of violence.

Although I was raised in one of the most violent slums in Europe, and possibly in the world, I find the idea of one person inflicting pain and injury on another, usually weaker, totally abhorrent. I remember with love my father who, although a man well capable of looking after himself, never raised a hand to me. I remember, with loathing, the so-called Christian Brothers of my approved school days, who practised their brand of Christianity by beating young boys practically senseless. In my many years on the streets as a criminal, and during the many senseless years spent in prison, I studiously avoided the use of violence. Only once did I break this code: when, as a hot-headed teenager, I laid out an uncle who was involved in an argument with my mother. I don't know who was the most surprised, the uncle, myself or my mother, who was furious that I should interfere in a family row between brother and sister. That assault arose from a deep-rooted family loyalty, in this case to my mother. Family ties in my life have been exceptionally strong, and I owe a great debt in particular to my womenfolk – my mother, my grandmother who was such a great influence of my early life, and later my wife, Betty.

Although it might surprise an outsider, this intense feeling for family is far from unusual among criminals. The roughest brawler in Glasgow will act with the greatest cap-doffing respect to a woman whose husband he has just pulverized. The same man might hand his wife a casual clout on a Friday night, but any outsider who laid an eye on her, much less a finger, would be in mortal danger. In my family, there were never any clouts, casual or not, for the womenfolk; for they, more than anyone, dominated family life. This attitude to women was reflected away from the home among the villains who were my friends and accomplices: apart from child-molesters, the very lowest form of criminal life, the men we held in the greatest contempt were the sex-offenders. I don't suppose I ever heard it said, but it was nevertheless implicitly accepted, that a man who used violence against a woman wasn't a man at all: to expose such a weakness of character made him unsuitable company among professional thieves. These feelings against violence, the importance of family ties, the strict regard for the proper treatment of womenfolk, were as strong as ever that Friday in 1969, as the foreman of the jury came to his feet.

Yet that day the High Court of Judiciary was to find me guilty of the brutal murder of a seventy-two year old woman. I knew the verdict was inevitable when the eight men and seven women of the jury came shiftily into court. I had suspected for the five days of the trial that the case against me was so strong that I would be convicted. But I still had a hopeless faith that the judicial process could not go so awry as to condemn an innocent man for the worst crime humanity knows. So I was overwhelmed with a crippling sense of outrage when the word was actually spoken: 'Guilty'.

My emotions were such a maelstrom of anger, bitterness, indignation and hopelessness that although I recall the mood with the greatest clarity, I still find it difficult to describe. I found myself saying to myself, 'Surely they *know* I am innocent – everyone *knows* I am not capable of such a monstrous act.' The dead lady in the case, Mrs Rachel Ross, wife of a wealthy bingo-hall owner, had been found bound, beaten and left injured for more than thirty hours, her life slowly ebbing away. Her husband too had been beaten and humiliated before giving his assailants the key to the safe in his house. Surely everyone in Scotland knew

13

– police, lawyers, judge and jury – just *knew* that I had never entered a private house, that I had never used violence during a crime, and that the mere thought of using violence against an old lady filled me with a cold horror. And why should I need to torture an old man to get the keys of a simple household safe? Wasn't I the man who, with a few ounces of gelignite or nitroglycerine, had tackled some of the toughest bank safes in Britain? I was a peterman, an artist, not a thug. Again I asked, surely they *know*?

They didn't, of course. The prosecution case had been too good, good almost to the point of perfection. It was overwhelmingly damning, and yet I had never been near that house in Ayr where old Mrs Ross was to face such a harsh and painful death: the evidence, in fact, was too good to be true.

Towering above me on the bench, Lord Grant, dressed in the scarlet and white robes of the Lord Justice Clerk, the second highest judge in Scotland, spoke in a voice still gruff from a recent throat operation:

'Patrick Connolly Meehan, there is only one sentence I can pass and that is imprisonment for life.'

From the gallery above came a woman's scream: 'He is innocent!' I realized why I was so outraged. Strangely, it was not so much that I had been wrongly convicted of murder, in itself a stunning blow for any man, perhaps the gravest injustice any society can inflict on one of its own. No, for some days I had been resigned to the fact that I was going to be labelled 'murderer'. It was as the judge was speaking that the source of the pain became clear: I had been *insulted*; grievously and terribly insulted.

To be wrongly convicted, even of murder, is the sort of risk a villain runs throughout his life, a risk he learns to live with. But to be convicted of a crime so hideous, to be branded throughout my native land as a vicious, merciless thug, was a blow that withered my soul. I knew, before the sentence had left Lord Grant's lips, that the rest of my days must be devoted to removing the stain. As I was escorted from the court, I turned to the jury and said: 'You have made a terrible mistake.'

In the cells below, Betty was sobbing hysterically, bordering on a state of collapse. Ignoring the police officers in my escort, she threw her arms round me, her tears wetting my cheeks. 'I know you didn't do it – I know you are not capable of it,' she choked. 'Always remember that, Paddy – I know you didn't do it.' I comforted her in my arms, just as her words had comforted me. Here was one less person I had to convince of my innocence – the most important person of all. Now all I had to do was to convince the people of Scotland, the judiciary and – the biggest hurdle of all – the politicians.

It was the beginning of a campaign which, as year passed year, was to be pushed and cajoled and battered from my solitary confinement cells through the Scottish Office to Whitehall, from Whitehall to the Houses of Parliament and, eventually, into Buckingham Palace itself. It was to be a long struggle . . .

There are some slums in the world whose very names are synonymous with crime and violence. Their names crop up in books, they are portrayed in the newspapers almost as if they are living creatures. You see them on film in the cinema and on television. People who come from these areas are automatically looked upon by more fortunate citizens with a combination of fear, hostility and curiosity.

There are slums like Hell's Kitchen in New York, breeding-ground for boxers and gangsters. There are the docks at Marseilles, where the French Connection was forged and Charles de Gaulle recruited the strong-arm 'guerrillas' he needed to fight the OAS. There are the backstreets of Macao, where illegal gold changes hand by the kilogramme, and the harbour in Hong Kong, where the trade is in opium and human flesh.

In my experience, Britain has few such places, ones which would figure in a 'world-class' league of squalor. True, the East End of London has seen its villains, and Cardiff's Tiger Bay and the Dingle in Liverpool have had their moments. There is, however, one area whose name stands out in the curiously inverted 'status' tables of tough neighbourhoods: the Gorbals, Glasgow. This is where I was born on August 12th, 1927.

The Gorbals, due in my childhood to achieve international infamy from the book *No Mean City*, was as poor and degraded a place as anywhere in Europe as The Depression swept the world. It was peopled mainly by embittered Irish Catholics, who had fled the hunger and never-ending civil disturbances of their homeland, only to find more hunger and more violence in Scotland – and not an emerald-green field in sight. In the two or three decades before the war, the Irish were joined in ever growing numbers by a people who suffered even more, the Jews fleeing the pogroms and persecutions of Eastern Europe. Although the slump had thrown thousands from the shipyards and the docks on the dole, the Jews, accustomed as they are to making the best of hard times, soon succeeded in establishing a modest prosperity – extremely modest by middle-class terms, but noticeably superior to the majority of their Scots-Irish neighbours.

I was fortunate, then, to grow up in Oxford Street, which was largely a Jewish area and somewhat insulated from the drunkenness, the brawling, the razor-fighting of the gangs of just a few streets away. 'A few streets away' was, in any case, a major voyage of discovery in my early childhood: children were not encouraged to stray far from home in the Gorbals. Not that they would have been in danger from any premeditated attack – tough as it was, I never remember a case of a child being molested – but there were too many incidents in which one could be accidentally involved: gang fights, police raids, scuffles with the odd group of Orangemen brave or drunk enough to stray into the place after a Celtic/Rangers football match.

I was extremely fortunate, too, in that I had a rare sort of father in Patrick Meehan, a man who was always in work. His work was always of the meanest kind, labouring in neighbouring foundries; but it was *work*, and to have it was just cause to make my mother, in her own way, a minor working-class snob. The benefits of a working father were lost on me, because it made me *different* and being different from your friends is an unforgivable sin among children. I didn't wear the parish suits – the dark grey flannels, all itchy and hairy, which were handed out to the children of the unemployed by the parish guardians. Nor did I have parish boots – a matter of considerable resentment.

'I just canna understand why you do it, when your daddy buys such lovely wee shoes,' I remember my mother Annie scolding during one of our few family rows.

I had come home for the second or third time wearing a pair of parish boots, sturdy scaled-down army-style boots with great

16

shining studs in the soles. I had swapped my shop-bought shoes for a pair of boots, much to the offence of my mother's gentle snobbery – after all, didn't a pair of shoes show the world that the family was not on the dole?

'It will save us a few shillin's,' I said. 'They're much stronger than the wee shoes and they'll last a lot longer.'

This may sound like a very adult thing for a child to say, and so it was, for I had heard it said several times before. It wasn't just *my* mother who was upset by my footwear-swapping ways: the mothers of the boys who received the shoes were also incensed. I had already received several long lectures on the sturdiness of parish boots. At this explanation, my mother gave me an old-fashioned look.

'I just canna understand why you set your heart to look just like all the poor children,' she said, as though we were actually rich.

'It's as I said, ma,' I repeated, 'they'll save us a few shillin's.'

I doubt she believed me, but I also doubt if she ever knew the real reason for my burning desire for parish boots. The answer lay in the steel studs. One of the few diversions for children in the Gorbals was to hang on the tail-end of lorries and carts to cadge a ride when they started off. We would be towed down the streets, whooping and yelling. In ordinary shoes, you stopped as soon as you let go of the lorry. With parish boots, you could carry on sliding for yards. I suppose those studs were the poor kid's answer to roller skates.

With a name like Patrick Connolly Meehan, no one will be surprised that the Irish rebel instinct was still very much alive in my family, and in fact we were related to James Connolly, the Irish socialist revolutionary. It was Connolly who led the march from Liberty Hall to take over the General Post Office in Dublin during the 1916 uprising. He was shot by the English – note I do not say by the British – an act which was never forgiven by my grandmother, Sabina, who was one of his many cousins. Sabina was a Fenian through and through, and she was to be one of the moulding influences of my childhood. One of my cousins, also called Paddy, was an orphan, and lived with my grandmother just round the corner. When I was five, it was decided I should go to live there, too, to keep him company. There was no great wrench involved – Sabina's home in South Portland Street was not more than a few yards away, and the family used both flats as communal property. Packy – renamed to avoid confusion – and I were to become firm friends and partners in innumerable exploits.

At my grandmother's, I received the great Irish brainwashing in Catholicism and rebellion. As a schoolboy, I knew all the rebel songs – I hardly knew of any other (I remember the existence of Bing Crosby coming as a great surprise to me when I was about eighteen). The flat was a place of deep conversations that went on into the early hours, of strange visitors who came and went, speaking with strong Irish accents. I have no doubt now – although I didn't know then – that these visitors were directly involved in the Troubles which were still going on over the water in Ulster, although the Free State had been in existence for fifteen years or more. My grandmother herself would go on mysterious journeys for a few days, returning secretive but elated. What she was involved in I do not know, but there was no secret that in her earlier days she and her husband, my grandfather, had been involved in the Duke Street shooting. This was told to me as one of the great epics of our time. A police waggon carrying Fenian prisoners was ambushed, the lock was shot off, and in the scuffle that followed a policeman was shot dead. My grandfather went on the run the same day. I suppose, thanks to my grandmother, I was ordained to be a rebel against society – although not in the way that she would have wished.

If I inherited anything from my grandmother, it was not so much her rabid Irish nationalism as her second line of interest, that of discovering new ways of making money. If there is a clash of interest between revolution and petty capitalism, my grandmother never accepted it. She had her finger in many pies, earning a shilling here and a shilling there, never in large amounts, but enough to combat the extremes of poverty. She would go to court to plead, convincingly, for some defendant's good character. She was also not above taking her small percentage from the opportunities created by the poverty of others. Many people, for instance, found it beyond their means to buy a whole sack of coal. Grandmother bought the sacks, and divided them into smaller amounts for sale. In some ways, I suppose, it was a social service

– a small amount of coal is better than no coal at all. Nevertheless, it was a service from which my grandmother reaped what
she considered to be a proper profit.

This quick eye for profit was soon adopted by Packy and me.
Living in the Jewish area offered one of the earliest opportunities, for we soon learned to exploit the possibilities of the Sab-
bath. Our neighbours followed their Orthodox faith with great
rigidity, forbidding themselves any sort of work on Saturdays.
Packy and I soon found that the simplest task – setting a match
to an already made fire, even switching a light on in some of the
strictest homes – could be worth a ha'penny; and a ha'penny
bought two gob-stoppers which really lived up to their name. As
if to prove, however, that we were not religious bigots, we
profited not only under the six-pointed Star of David, but
also within the shadow of the Cross. Every Sunday, Packy and I
were sent off to Mass, clutching in our well-scrubbed hands two
ha'pennies each. One was to buy a candle to burn for the soul of
Packy's dead mother – a duty we never shirked. The other was
for the collection plate. By a deft shuffling of the coins already on
the plate and a well-practised piece of legerdemain, we found we
could satisfy the piercing inspection of our neighbouring wor-
shippers and still pocket the ha'pennies. These, too, we quickly
converted into gob-stoppers and, after one clout from grandmother, learned the basic lesson of removing the evidence. We
were stupid enough one day to go home with a halo of sugary
toffee round our mouths. We only did it once – from then on,
the painstaking cleaning of faces after our illicit gob-stoppers
was probably the most gruelling act of personal hygiene we
underwent in a week.

Few young people, or older people lucky enough to have spent
their childhoods in happier neighbourhoods, are likely to understand the satisfaction of those gob-stopper escapades. Certainly,
we enjoyed the sweets with all the relish of every child who has
ever lived, but to us they were actually the bonus. The pleasure,
the secret fulfilment, lay in the schemes we had plotted working
out as planned. In other words, it was the means, not the end,
that were the spur.

Was this the beginning of a criminal mind? Years later, I was
often to ponder what gave me the greatest satisfaction: the

money from the bank safe or the fact that I had blown the safe so sweetly? During those years of childhood, however, such philosophizing never troubled our heads. It was the way of life in the Gorbals: getting your pleasures by manipulating or beating the system. In all truth, there was little else to do. The Catholic Church did its best, but also exacted its dues. There was a youth club in our neighbourhood, with a few table-tennis tables and a boxing ring. To get in, you had to be a regular attender at Mass, and even then you were subjected to a severe grilling by the mountain of a priest who guarded the door. Eventually, the indignity of pleasing the dog-collared doorkeeper outweighed the few pleasures the club had to offer. I now realize that to boycott the club was my first rebellion against the Church. Instead, we turned to other pleasures of the streets, for there was always something going on to send the adrenalin gushing.

Midsummer was a time for great fun and games, as the Orangemen began building up to their great march to celebrate July the 12th and the victory of a Dutch Protestant Prince over a Scottish Catholic King on an Irish riverbank more than two centuries previously. Much is made of the Catholic-Protestant hatreds in Glasgow but, in all honesty, I have to admit that they never made any deep impression on me. For a start, I hardly knew any Protestants and, anyway, I found their fife and drum bands distinctly stirring as they marched by – the Devil is supposed to have all the best tunes, but if so, he has loaned out a good few to the Orange Order.

Nevertheless, July was still a time for ambushing the marchers, hiding behind walls or up 'closes' – the Glasgow name for alleyways – with a few bottles or half-bricks ready to hand. We would wait until the head of the procession had passed before darting out, hurling our missiles, and disappear into the maze of the Gorbals as fast as we could run. We were never caught, I am glad to say, because we would have taken a severe beating. But did I hate Protestants? No – I don't think so, despite my grandmother's teachings. I threw stones at them because everyone else threw stones at them. It was part of childhood's calendar, like Christmas or birthdays. And anyway, it was exciting.

For a more regular diet of thrills, there was always Doyle's pub on a Saturday night. Doyle's, standing right on Gorbals Cross, was the toughest pub in an area of tough pubs, a place with the reputation to match a saloon in Dodge City. If word went round, 'Irish Gerry is out', Gorbals Cross was the place to be just after closing time on Saturday night. We children, too young to be in the pub to watch the action, would make our way down early in the evening, and knock on the doors of the houses overlooking the Cross. If we were early enough, the occupants would allow a grandstand position at the bedroom windows. We would sit, chattering impatiently, as the hours to closing time crawled snail-like by. Then it would happen. Doyle's door would burst open, and out onto the pavement would stagger Irish Gerry, one of the biggest men I have ever seen. He would peel off his jacket, stand swaying in his vest, and shout, 'I'm ready – come and get me you bastards.' Round the corner they would come, a patrol of six bobbies, their truncheons already drawn. The betting was on how many it would take tonight – how many bobbies that is. The fight would start without delay, fists and boots and truncheons flying, helmets spinning dizzily across the pavements. One or two bobbies would always go down, sometimes three or four. Then this seething intertwined mass of humanity would roll wildly to the open doors of the waiting Black Maria.

The biggest cheer I ever heard on Gorbals Cross was the night when the police van finally started on its journey to Nicholson Street police station, only to screech to a sudden halt fifty yards on.

Out of the *front* door hurtled the driver, followed closely by a triumphant Gerry, his arms held in the air with all the joy of a prize-fighter who had just won a world championship. Then, meekly, he got back into the van to be driven off to his inevitable fate. I never did find out how Gerry did that, for he must have overpowered the bobbies in the back, battered his way through the partition which separated the van from the cab, and then tackled the driver.

Once a month, Irish Gerry got his thirty days for assaulting the police, and we would have to serve out his sentence with him, waiting anxiously for the next episode of the Battle of Gorbals Cross. No one was ever seriously hurt, and the police seemed to take it, like Gerry, in good heart. Perhaps they used him as a one-man crash course in unarmed combat. No Mean City, they called Glasgow in those days.

As a child, of course, I had no reason to know that life was any different the world over.

2 Apprentice in crime

The trouble was, the Orange marches only occupied a couple of weeks a year, and even Irish Gerry could only keep us occupied one evening a month. That left a lot of days and nights in a year to fill, and there were few facilities in the Gorbals to keep an active young boy's interest. As far as I know, all young boys have an irresistible urge to climb things. The lucky ones have mountains, or at least trees. Packy and I had neither, so we made do with the next best thing – buildings. And as occupiers tend to make objections to young boys shinning over their slates, it was natural that we should turn our attentions to empty buildings, of which the neighbourhood had a great store. The slump had closed many offices and warehouses. Others were empty simply because they were so dilapidated that they might fall in on any inhabitants. For agile hands and feet and prying eyes, there was a whole treasure trove of mysterious places to explore in peace.

My first 'crime' was committed in total innocence. Exploring an empty warehouse one day at the age of eight, we came across an office full of rotting furniture. Remembering the steady profits that my grandmother made selling small amounts of coal in an area constantly starved of fuel, we decided to go into the firewood business. We broke up a few drawers which, as far as we were aware, neither belonged to nor interested any living being. We began to sell our bundles around the streets at a penny a time.

Within days, the big horny hands of PC John Young, our local bobby, fell on my shoulder. 'Where did you get the wood son?' he asked in his kindly way, and in my innocence I told him. A few days later, I walked silently with my father across the Stockwell Bridge over the Clyde to the Central Police Court. My father, a strong but quiet man, accepted the situation with no more than a sad shake of the head. I had expected a thrashing, and no doubt deserved one, but my father refused to break his lifelong principle of not using violence on his children. In many ways, I wish he had, for a good hiding would have been easier

23

to bear than the sadness in his eyes. The walk to court that day was not a happy occasion.

He stood by my side as I was taken before the magistrates. PC Young, to his credit, spoke up for me, saying that he was sure I had stolen the wood not realizing it was someone else's property. He was a good copper – unlike many I was to meet later in life. He did his duty as he saw it, but I gained the distinct impression that sometimes it caused him pain. I was admonished, the least serious punishment in Scottish law. However, at the age of eight, I was now the possessor of a police record. Because of the hurt I had caused my father, and perhaps in no little way because of the fairness of the treatment I had received from John Young, I resolved to 'go straight'. I hadn't, of course, heard that phrase then, but I was determined not to get into more trouble. It was not to be.

The very desire to keep away from empty buildings and their temptations caused Packy and me one day to make the long walk to Queen's Park, the only open space available to my neighbourhood – and that was liberally sprinkled with 'Keep off the Grass' notices. It did, however, have trees which, as I have already said are specifically designed for little boys to climb. I was practising my Tarzan swing along a branch when it broke, pitching me to the ground. Sadly, for me and for future generations of Scottish law officers, my audience included two plainclothes CID men. I would have thought, given the Glasgow of the 1930s, they would have had better things to do, but no. These two hulking detectives pulled off a lightning arrest which, I hope, reflected great credit in their records. I was escorted to the Southern police office on a charge of malicious damage. I was admonished yet again, but my 'record' doubled its length virtually overnight. I left court that day with no feelings of gratitude towards the police. If the die were not irredeemably cast then, and I suspect it was, only another year was to pass before my induction into the ranks of full-time criminals.

It was perhaps an unwise thing for my grandmother to do, but I think I can understand her motives. She bought Packy a bicycle, but there was no money for one for me. Her reasoning no doubt was that Packy, as an orphan, had missed many of the greater joys of life and the bike was meant as a tiny compensa-

24

tion. To me of course the situation was unbearable: Packy, my inseparable companion, would leave me, floated away on the magic carpet of Raleigh wheels. I would be left behind, alone and forlorn. I think any other child in the Gorbals would have done what I did, given these c..cumstances. I went out and stole a bike. I couldn't, of course, show my new prize to the family, so I hid it every evening in a nearby 'dunny' – a basement cellar common to all Glasgow tenements, used for storing rubbish and fuel; and scene, no doubt, of the conception of many a Glaswegian.

The sight of young Paddy Meehan riding a bike through the streets could not be kept a secret long. One day as I furtively dragged my new prize from the dunny, the police who had been waiting pounced. This time, there would be no admonishment. Once again, my father accompanied me, but this time, because of the seriousness of the charge, I was to appear before the Sheriff. With two previous convictions – 'theft' and 'malicious damage' must have sounded ugly words to people unaware of the previous circumstances – there was no doubt as to the result. It was approved school for me. Outside the court, my father tried to climb into the car which was to take me to Slatefield Approved School. He was pushed away roughly. 'We're in charge of your son now,' someone said, and we drove away. He stood on the pavement, his shoulders stooped. For the first time I felt real guilt, not because of any crime I had committed, but at the pain I kept inflicting on my father. The feeling was soon to change to one of outrage.

My arrival at Slatefield brought me into contact with a body of men I hate more than any other single group I have ever met – the so-called Christian Brothers. While it is impossible to generalize by condemning the entire order – there were some good ones – I have never met more bullies under one banner in my life. They taught with the Bible in one hand, and a belt in the other, and it was the belt which got the greatest use.

My first meeting was fairly typical of the breed. They took my clothes, handed me a parish suit – I had got one at last! – and then a Brother marched me to a bathroom. As he explained the rules, he barked: 'Stand to attention while I am talking to you.' I didn't even know what standing to attention meant, and I must have swayed, because the next minute his great fist swung through the air like a piston, hitting me on the side of the head and half-knocking me to the floor. It was the first time in my life that an adult had ever laid a hand on me, and it was the hand of a hulking Irishman some six feet tall and probably fourteen stones in weight. The hearing had gone from one ear, I could feel my cheek already swelling, but it was not the physical hurt that worried me. My pride had been outraged. That blow was the first of many, designed presumably to break my spirit and make me conform to the rules. The effect was the diametric opposite.

From that day, I have never accepted the authority of another man over me. From that day, I have dismissed the teachings of the Roman Catholic Church. No doubt the Brother left me in the bathroom that day thinking, 'That's another one taught a lesson.' He could not have been more wrong. As soon as he closed the door, I donned my parish suit, opened the window, dropped to the ground and set off for home.

My father, understandably, had stopped for a couple of pints on the way home to drown his sorrows. He was somewhat bemused to find me sitting there when he arrived – and outraged when I told him of the Christian Brother who had clouted me. He was all for keeping me at home, but my mother would not hear of it. Next day, she delivered me back to Slatefield.

The Christian Brothers did not restrict themselves to individual brutality to break a boy. They also had a system of collective blackmail designed to single out a rebel and separate him from his fellows. At Slatefield, to abscond meant to bring down a collective punishment on the entire school. Privileges for all were stopped for a week, privileges like sixpence a week pocket-money or being allowed to listen to the radio in the evenings. The absconder was made to run the gauntlet of the whole school – some sixty-eight of them – while the boys aimed kicks at his legs and backside. The other boys were supposed to be angered by their loss of privileges, and therefore happy to land hefty kicks. If this mass psychology didn't work, a Brother stood by to punch any boy he didn't think was showing enough enthusiasm for kicking a friend black and blue. Believe it or not, the gauntlet was an 'unofficial' punishment, staged, I think, for no other reason than this Brother's love of blood-sports. The official punishment for absconding was the 'shifters' – a public beating with a specially-made leather strap some two feet long, three inches wide and reinforced with a band of pliable wire stitched down the centre. The rules for shifters were laid down by whatever body was responsible for running Slatefield. I assume there was such a body, but I never saw any results of its stewardship. The maximum number of strokes, for instance, was supposed to be twelve.

As a boy who created something of a record by enduring shifters on his second day there, I was soon to learn that a mere dozen of the best was nowhere near enough for one Brother, whom I have since dubbed 'Brother Bligh'. His lust for public floggings was shared by the hapless captain of the *Bounty*. The good Brother 'bent' the shifters rules. The strokes were delivered, before the assembled school, while the victim touched his toes – and continued to touch his toes as the blows landed. I can think of few things more likely to make a boy stand bolt upright than a two-foot-long strap curling round his backside, a natural reaction which Brother Bligh exploited to the full. When I snapped erect, the stroke that had just landed simply didn't count. In this way, I had lost track at thirty before the punishment finally ended. I didn't cry – how could I, in front of more than sixty boys? – and that was a piece of self-control of which I still feel proud. Perhaps it was my stubborn refusal to give way to tears that forced my tormentor to go on.

I cried that night in the dormitory, keeping my head under the blankets in a vain attempt to smother the sobs. 'There's no need to be ashamed of yourself,' came a voice down the room, 'we all have to cry at some time or other.' Perhaps I have been offensive by using that Brother Bligh nickname to the memory of the good Captain. After all, he was a remarkable sailor. And he only flogged mature men, not nine year old boys, away from home for the first night of their lives.

I could go on and on about approved schools, but I see little point in repeating an almost endless list of beatings, punches, kicks and other brutalities. In seven years, I was moved endlessly from one to another, constantly absconding – I think I went on the run ten or twelve times in all. Sometimes I would go back to my grandmother's home because, with her lifelong antipathy to 'the authorities' she would refuse policemen entry without a warrant. The police, unwilling to go through the processes of getting a warrant for such a minor quarry, would simply wait until I was out on the streets one day and pick me up.

It is significant that the only happy time I remember of the period was nearly two years in a Protestant school in Oakbank, Aberdeen. There, the Governor, Mr McLeod, had a real understanding of an adolescent's need to express himself in some positive way or another and eventually I was promoted to head gardener. I might even have considered reforming there – presumably the object of such institutions – had it not been for an unfortunate coincidence concerning an attractive young girl and a happy old lady.

To explain, the school allowed us some freedom and we could walk into town and have a cup of tea in a local cafe. There I met the first love of my life, a young lassie who wanted to become a school teacher. It was never a serious affair, but it was as important to me as only young love can be. I was acutely conscious of my situation, an approved school boy meeting a highly respectable young woman, and I became determined to show that I could compete with any of the more eligible local lads. That meant paying for the cups of coffee and the cakes which were the 'cover' for our meetings. I had no money, obviously, but soon found a relatively innocuous way of raising some. I must have had green fingers, for my efforts had that year produced an abundance of vegetables, including a particularly good crop of onions. There were far more onions than the school needed, and many looked like running to seed. I acquired a few and sold them door to door in the area.

Either my onions were too good, or the prices I was charging were too low – probably the latter, this being Aberdeen! – for one old lady decided that here was a supply of produce which must be encouraged. She went along to Oakbank, knocked on the front door, and asked: 'Could I have some more of your lovely onions, please?' I can only guess at the reaction of the staff, for I didn't wait round to face the music. Tipped off by a friend who heard the doorstep exchange, I was on the first train to Glasgow. It was the end of Oakbank, the end of the girl in the tea shop (I hope she has had a happier life than me) and in all probability the end of the one last chance I had of adjusting to the life of an ordinary citizen.

It was after this escape, I think – there were so many they have become a little confused after all these years – that my grandmother's 'Irish Connection' was exploited. I found myself on a ferry to Belfast, and spent six months in a household of IRA sympathizers in Co Antrim. Those months gave me a lot of time to think, for there was little else to do. For obvious reasons, I could not go to school and I had to be wary of going out a great deal; for a youth with a strong Glasgow accent was very conspicuous in a small Ulster town. My thoughts sealed my future. It appeared to my youthful logic that I had been in a hell of a lot of trouble for very little profit. I had been taken from my home and a family which cared; I had been deprived of my liberty for nigh on seven years; I had been insulted, bullied and beaten. And for what? Apart from the bicycle – which, I admitted, had been a real theft – my ill-gotten gains mounted up to a few bundles of firewood that no one else had wanted, and a couple of dozen onions which would have ended on the compost heap anyway. My only 'victim' was the branch of a tree in Queen's Park. Yet I had met youths in approved schools whose pockets, on the 'outside', had bulged with money and cigarettes, whose arms had never lacked a pretty young girl, all won from the proceeds of crime. If anything, they had received better treatment than me inside. It was a sheep or a lamb situation, I reasoned. I might as well let crime pay! The first course of action, I decided, was to end my approved school days which, under the system which then applied, would have kept me under supervision until the age of eighteen and then fed me straight into the army.

I returned to Glasgow with the avowed plan of being sent to Borstal; a strange plan the reader might think, but one thought out by young criminal brains which have given more thought to the future than me. The advantage of the Borstal system was that it carried a fixed-time limit: ten months, and you were released. As a youth of sixteen, it offered me a year's 'remission' over the approved schools; and although Borstal was supposed to be tougher, I judged that I could suffer no more than I had at the hands of the Christian Brothers. How did I get to Borstal? Quite the simplest thing I have ever done. I stole some oxy-acetylene equipment from a Glasgow garage and allowed myself to get caught. Then I confessed that I had planned to raid a safe in the office at a nearby scrapyard.

The police helped me along, for they knew my Borstal ambition as well as I did – it was a well-trodden path for many of my generation. 'Do you know anything about a break-in at such and such store?' they asked. 'Yes,' I said, 'I did it.' 'Do you know anything about the factory job at so and so?' they asked. 'Yes,' I said, 'I did that too.' Then they helped me write my statement, confessing to crimes I knew nothing about. They told me how I was supposed to have entered the building, described the loot that was missing, and together we concocted a story to say how I got rid of the stuff. They knew, of course, that I was completely innocent, but they also knew I wanted to make Borstal a dead certainty. They were happy to be improving their detection figures, by 'solving' unsolved crimes. It seemed an equitable arrangement at the time.

So off I went to Polmont, near Falkirk, for my ten months Borstal training. As I had guessed, it held no terrors for me, a hardened veteran of the Christian Brothers' machine. It was even quite useful: they gave me a course in welding, a handy trade for a wouldbe safe-cracker. My ten months completed without too much trouble, I was back on the streets of Glasgow a free man: or rather, a very grown-up youth. The law-makers hadn't meant it, of course, but they had given me a superb training for my chosen career. Paddy Connolly Meehan had finished his apprenticeship with honours. It was time to put his trade to work.

3 Peterman

I suppose most people think that a man turns to crime because he is too lazy, or too stupid, to make a good living legitimately.

That may be true of some, but they tend to be the ones who profit little and who suffer the most. To become a *good* villain – an 'earner' – takes as much thought, as much preparation, as much skill and a good deal more nerve than anything in straight society. The risks, the satisfaction of the rebellion against authority, are as big a reward as the cash. In my late teens, crime represented a glittering opportunity. I was not to learn until much later – far too late – that as a lifestyle it almost inevitably ends in bitterness, frustration and despair. There may be 'Mr Bigs' who always get away with it – but I don't know any. We all become familiar with the inside of a cell at some time or another. These thoughts, however, were far from my mind as the war in Europe neared its end, bringing in a new area of opportunity for black-marketeers, spivs and thieves in general. It was a time of 'shortages'; and the public, who had been prepared to suffer loyally during the worst of the hostilities, wanted some of the spoils of the approaching victory. Many of them could only be gained illegally. It was a time of great change for me.

I had learned that, as a man marked by the police, I had to have some 'visible means of support' if I were to launch into criminal activities without constant harassment, so I put my trade as a welder to use. It meant 'working' day and night – at my two different skills – but I had at last realized that the main object of crime was not so much to steal things, but to steal things without getting caught.

My first job after Borstal didn't add to my respect for authority, for it brought me face to face with yet another 'racket' run by the so-called forces of law and order, the officially approved 'sweat-shop'. My aftercare officer found me a job at a nearby firm of constructional engineers, an act of welfare for which – at first – I was duly grateful. When I discovered that my pay of one shilling an hour was not much more than a third of men doing

31

the same work, my gratitude cooled a little. It was not until I had a row with the boss's son, who picked on me continually thinking I had no right to fight back, that I discovered that the aftercare officer was a close friend of the workshop manager and often introduced cheap labour to the company. I left and went to work in the ship-yards.

During this period, I picked up my first and only conviction for violence. As I have already described, an uncle started a row with my mother which left her in tears. Walking in to find my mother sobbing, I lost my temper and punched him a few times. His wife's complaint to the police – the uncle himself agreed to forget it – earned me thirty days for common assault.

Outside again, I found a way of turning the end-of-war short-ages to a handsome profit. They were small, light, difficult to trace, and the big stores held them in their thousands. They were called – remember? – clothing coupons. They could have been invented to satisfy a villain's dreams. Scrupulously honest people, who wouldn't dream of handling stolen property in the normal sense, made an exception for clothing coupons. It was probably the nearest Britain ever came to the American 'speakeasy' system, when sales of booze hit record level during Prohibition. Like the society ladies of America slurping away at their illicit gin, the wealthy ladies of Glasgow were quite happy to pay two shillings a time for the coupons, passport to a little glamour after the drab years of 'utility' frocks. 'It isn't really illegal, is it my dear?' they must have said over the Crown Derby. 'Just sort of *bending* the rules a little.' Clothing coupons satisfied all my criteria for a successful job. They were held by the big stores, which were rarely attended at night, so there was little risk of being surprised. At the beginning, at least, they were rarely locked away – the money was in the safe, but the coupons were in the office drawer. And when it was often possible to lift as many as eight or ten thousand in a night, at two shillings a time, the pickings were pretty good.

During the day, I was still working in the ship-yards, picking up one-and-ninepence an hour as a trainee welder – plus the perks. I would help the trained men out with their piece work schedules, or even do their full shift if they decided to 'jump the wall' – sign in at the works office, and leave over the wall to take

32

a day off. They would slip me five shillings or so at the end of the week, not an inconsiderable sum in those days. All in all, things were going pretty well . . . until one night I walked out of a store, my bag bulging with clothing coupons, straight into the law. They had found our car, become suspicious and waited for us with open arms.

I was out on bail, awaiting trial, when I dodged into a close one night to shelter from the rain. Taking advantage of the same shelter was a stunningly attractive red-head. We began to talk. Her name turned out to be Betty Carson, which is as good a Protestant name as you will ever find. Lord Carson, who raised the Ulster Volunteer Force to keep Ulster out of the Irish Free State, is as much a hero to Orangemen as James Connolly is to Republicans. I am delighted to say that we were both far too sensible to pay any heed to Glasgow's traditions of sectarian hatred. We had enough problems without the priests getting involved. I could hardly have looked a good prospect for Betty. I was still only eighteen, but already had a growing reputation as a local villain. Even worse, I was awaiting trial on a serious charge and neither of us had any doubt that I would be going away for a long time. Betty, five-feet-four-inches of fighting spirit, knew in her head she was letting herself in for a lot of tears. But as happens in these matters, her heart decided to take the risk. We told no one of our courtship – I was terrified her parents would intervene and break up the relationship – and after five months we married. The ceremony took place on September 20th, 1945 at the John Knox Church, not a usual venue for a good Catholic boy. In the event, no one raised any objections although I have no doubt my grandmother, who had died in 1942, must have turned in her grave.

In a matter of weeks, I was sent down for fifteen months, not an auspicious start to a marriage. Emotionally, I was a strange mixture of young and old, the bright eyed young lover struggling with my own determination to be a man in the eyes of other men – and few people can have mixed with a tougher bunch of men. I was still a teenager, but well on the way to being an old lag. I was also a married man.

I can think of no better reason for a young girl to condemn for ever the husband who leaves her in the predicament in which I left Betty, and yet her loyalty remained a total commitment. In the youthful arrogance of those days, I failed to realize what an appalling sacrifice I was forcing upon her. Had I realized, perhaps I would have made decisions there and then which would have turned my life to a less erratic and dangerous course. But that is speaking with hindsight: my determination to be as hard as, if not harder, than any other Gorbals hard-man just wouldn't allow such sentimentality.

She wore green the day I came out, the first of a whole series of green suits and dresses and coats which – depending on the time of the year – she would don to greet me at the gates of far too many prisons. She said the green set off the depth of her fiery red hair. I believe that eventually for her, green came to be symbolic of my all-too-rare periods of freedom. And anyway, the colour in her hair was to fade over the years, hastened I have no doubt by the worry and distress I was to pile onto her. That first reunion just before seven AM in the shadow of the stifling walls of Barlinnie jail, was to set a pattern which rarely changed. She would greet me smiling and laughing, with babbling talk about the future. I realize now she probably 'babbled' to hide her fear of the inevitable question: 'How long will it last this time . . . ?'

I suppose most sensible couples celebrate their special occasions over a good steak and a bottle of wine with a little soft music and romantic lighting. Our background music was the empty thud of a prison gate closing, our first kiss taking place to an orchestra of early morning traffic as grey people made their way to their grey workplaces. We would walk hand in hand through the streets of Glasgow to our flat, where our celebratory meal would be a huge plate of ham and eggs. She always cooked a hearty breakfast. I was always unable to eat it. The excitement of release, the anxiety about the future, the months – and later years – of numb acceptance of prison stodge making it impossible for me to eat so richly.

We would stay in the flat all day, getting to know each other once again. In later years, there were the children to play with – and get to know again. In the evenings, we would visit some of Betty's relations for cups of tea and ham sandwiches and cakes. Her family, strangely, became very important to me. Hardworking, clean-living folk, they accepted me because they realized it would be impossible to reject me without also rejecting Betty. They would talk about anything under the sun except crime and prison. But at the end of the evening, as the dishes were being dried, one of them would say, 'I hope you're going to stay out this time, Paddy . . .' I promised I would and they accepted my promises solemnly. They probably doubted me inwardly, but they were good people and always willing to give a man a chance to live up to his word. I feel ashamed that I let them down, too. On the second day after my release, I would go out and get drunk. My old cronies would be happy to see me again . . .

As it turned out over the years my relationship with Betty was to be one of the few highlights of my life. She was a fine mother to my children, a marvellous companion, and full of cheer in even the gloomiest circumstances. It was not to be a conventional marriage. She was eventually to divorce me, jaded by years of my 'going away', but the divorce was little more than a technicality. I still lived with her when I was free, and it was as a divorcee that she played the leading part in the campaign against the murder conviction.

The Victorian pile of Barlinnie jail, Glasgow, is never a happy place. A cold dampness hangs over the place, the sort of atmosphere that can rot a man's spirit as well as his bones. The damp mingles with the stench of the 'mopping-out buckets' – the lavatory pails which stand in each cell – and the inevitable institutional smell of boiled cabbage and men living together in too close proximity. In those months after the war, an extra flavour of horror was added to the general foreboding by a rash of executions. There had been no hangings for many years – there had been no cases serious enough to justify the imposition of the death penalty – but I was unlucky enough to be an inmate of D-Hall when several men walked to the noose.

One was John Lyons, who killed an innocent sailor in a gang fight. Another was Paddy Caracher, one of the toughest men ever to enter a Scottish jail, who was said to have struggled all the way to the gallows. From my cell in D-Hall, I could hear the thump as the trap opened and a man fell to his death. The silence that descends on a prison after a hanging is the most fearful thing I have ever experienced. But for some enlightened legislation, although I could not know it then, such a silence would have been my own epitaph. For make no mistake, but for the abolition of capital punishment, I would have joined the ranks of Timothy Evans and possibly James Hanratty, dying at the end of a rope for a murder I did not commit.

I was out again in 1947 and went back to work in the shipyards. There, for the first time, I met a man who took politics seriously. I shall call him Peter although that is not his real name, for he is still alive and I do not wish to cause him any embarrassment. We would work side by side high up on the shell butts – the V joints of a ship's hull – welding plates, and found we had much in common. We had both suffered the poverty, the degradation, the hopelessness of the Gorbals and both of us had known despair. We had, however, decided upon different escape routes. Until meeting Peter, I had known of only two methods of combating the misery of slum life. One was the Roman Catholic way, to endure a barren life cheerfully accepting that it was merely a probationary period for a happy hereafter. This, the Opium-of-the-Masses approach, I dismissed forcefully and set about upon my individual escape route, financed from the proceeds of crime. Peter, a man some twenty years older than me, had decided upon a much more idealistic course: he would not escape alone, but would take all his fellow sufferers with him. He was an ardent Communist, determined to change society on pure Marxist lines. He was as genuine a man as I have ever met, totally committed to his beliefs. I think I have made it clear he made a big impression on me.

Under his influence, I began reading Marx, Engels, Lenin. I was an easy convert, for there was no need to convince me about the exploitation of the working classes. At lunchtimes, Peter would carry a soap box to the yard gates, and preach his particular gospel to anyone who would stand and listen. I took to joining him, going round the crowd selling copies of *The Daily Worker*. But Peter was a gentle man in action, although his speeches glowed red hot, and I was a young and impatient twenty year old with a lot of lost time to make up. I needed excitement, action, and an instant change in my living standards. And clothes were still rationed.

I already had a prime target in mind . . . a clothing warehouse which I knew to be bulging with those tiny little scraps of paper worth two shillings a time. It took me only two hours to break into the 'dunny' – the basement cellar – and cut a way through the wall into the warehouse. Creeping upstairs to the office, I suffered my first setback: there was nothing to be had except a large safe. Clothing coupon thefts had become too much of an easy thing: the police had started persuading trades people to lock them away with the cash. I needed Andy, one of the best petermen in Glasgow, an aristocrat of the local underworld. With a coolness I now find difficult to believe, I put down my tools, left the building and began to scour the local pubs looking for my man.

It didn't take long. Glasgow villains are men of habit – a blessing for the CID – and within the hour Andy was carefully prodding gelignite into the keyhole with a broken off knitting needle. It was a beautiful job, a peach. Within minutes, we were out on the street again, weighed down with coupons and cash. If that's all there is to blowing a safe, I thought, then that's the job for me. I set about to learn the trade of peterman. It is not a job you can study at night-school and no one has printed any textbooks on the subject, so I went for my information to the fountain head, cracksmen like Andy and – in Scotland at least – the father-figure of them all, Johnny Ramensky.

John, a Glaswegian born of Lithuanian parents, was a story-book villain. His skills were lauded even by the police, so much so that they eventually led him into one of the strangest episodes in the history of the British army. During the war, he had been parachuted behind the lines to crack enemy safes containing top-secret information. For his pains, he was awarded the Distinguished Conduct Medal – a *conduct* medal for a professional thief! All is fair, so they say . . . With mentors like this, and a certain aptitude for quick learning, I was soon to be a master craftsman.

Now I would like to make it clear that any fool can blow a safe. Given an undisturbed entry into the building of choice and a few ounces of gelignite, a trained chimpanzee could do the job. He could also blow up the contents of the safe, the office, the building, his accomplices, himself . . . and probably knock the hinges off the door of a police station 200 yards away. The secret is to open the safe with as little damage and as little noise as possible.

First I learned the types of safe and their weaknesses, makes like Ratner's, Milner's, Hobbs and Hart's, which no longer exist. I learned how to pack the keyholes with gelignite or if it were a combination lock how to chisel off the dial, knock the spindle through, and how to pack the hole that remained. I learned to tie a long piece of string to the handle – so that I could find it again after the bang – and how a safe door always blows off in the direction of the hinges. This is vital: it is the easiest thing in the world to blow the safe door right through a window and out into the street. This tends to arouse some curiosity among passers-by. If the hinges are pointing towards a window, the safe must be moved, and ordinary car-jacks are the tools which are used. Car-jacks were to play a significant part in my life later on. One always covers the safe with carpets or sacking or anything else that is available, to deaden the noise, and it is essential to remove any likely projectile, such as the keyhole cover, or the manufacturer's nameplate.

One man I met in Barlinnie ignored this advice – to his cost. On his release, he set up a safe job and everything went well until the bang. He felt a shattering pain in his chest and, looking down, saw blood surging through his clothes. Trying to control his panic, he walked from the building and got as far away as possible before he collapsed in the road. Naturally, the police were interested to know how he had come by this unusual chest injury. He had been stabbed, he told them, by an assailant he did not recognize. The police were less than impressed by the story when, during an emergency operation, the surgeon muttered 'Hello, hello, hello, what's this?' and held up the safe's keyhole cover. I have heard of people being caught in possession of the evidence, but that's ridiculous.

Safe-blowing is an extremely dangerous profession and I shudder now at the risks I once took. Gelignite, which we bought from miners in the pits south of Glasgow, is no toy, but there was a time when even that did not satisfy me. Nitro-glycerine, the most explosive component of gelignite, is a liquid and that has major attractions for a peterman – it can be dripped gently into a lock, which saves a lot of finicky packing. Nitro is, of course, notoriously unstable. Films have been made about it – remember *The Wages of Fear*? I produced it by melting down gelignite in a frying pan, over a gentle flame on an ordinary kitchen stove (not my stove, incidentally: we always chose an unoccupied house for obvious reasons). Any man who makes his living frying gelignite must be either totally fearless, totally lacking in imagination or totally insane. I will leave the reader to judge in my case. My earnest advice to anyone is to leave gelignite or nitro strictly alone, and take up a safe occupation like motor-racing or rock-climbing. Only once in my life was nitro of real use . . . and that was to rid myself of a notorious pest.

As my reputation as a cracksman began to spread, I gained a certain notoriety in the Glasgow underworld. That inevitably attracted the attentions of hangers-on. One was a man whose sight was so bad that he wore huge 'bottle-top' spectacles, whose nerves were so bad that most of his beer missed his mouth and went down his shirt, and yet he wanted to blow safes. One night in the pub, anxious to be rid of his attentions, a friend and I admitted we were going out on a job. As he had no record, would he like to carry the stuff? At first he flushed with pride, but when we strapped a bottle of clear liquid under his armpit, he began to pale.

'Wha . . . wha . . . what is it?' he asked, his hands twitching even more than usual.

'It's only nitro,' we said, calmly. 'You'll be all right so long as you treat it carefully.'

We told him to meet us at Glasgow Central Station – he thought that was the target, a railway station packed with travellers! – and we steered him into the night. Finishing our drinks, we ran from the pub, went round the block, and waited. We saw him coming down the street walking like a man on stilts, arms jammed by his sides, the lamp-light flashing in his spectacle lenses as his head screwed nervously from side to side. As he reached the corner, my mate, Ted Martin, a hulking figure of a man, pushed out as though running to catch a train, smashed into our friend with the force of a rugby half-back and knocked him to the ground.

The hysterical screams stopped traffic for hundreds of yards. He lay on his back his arms and legs flailing like an upturned beetle, and he didn't stop screaming until he heard our laughter.

The bottle contained water, of course. He never spoke to me again. There were a few laughs in those days, but the supply was beginning to run dry.

As Christmas 1947 began to approach, I felt the need for some extra cash – I thought Betty deserved a few treats as compensation for living with a rogue like me. Our baby, Pat, was a couple of months old. The trouble with doing your Christmas shopping with gelignite is that the 'holiday' can last a lot longer than you expect. I was arrested after blowing the safe of a large grocery store in Bedford Street, and lifting £150, the weekend takings and a fair amount of money in those days. I brought in the New Year of 1948 facing three years' penal servitude. Betty, to say the least, was not happy with her Hogmanay present.

There will perhaps be people who will accuse me of trying to glamorize those early days as a safe-blower. I can assure them nothing is further from my mind. I have tried, as honestly as I can, to recapture the excitements I felt then, the excitements that must come to any young man who has chosen a career and then finds he is quite good at the work.

I was good at the work, yes. But I was not *successful* because I kept getting caught. It is one thing to be the centre of attention in a pub, to be bought drinks by total strangers anxious to bask in some inverted form of reflected glory. It is another to look into the eyes of a woman you dearly love, knowing that you are to be taken away, leaving her to fend for herself and your child, in one of the toughest cities in an unkind world. That's why the man who goes out, day in day out, to a job he hates, to put food on the family table and shoes on the children's feet, is the real hero. I loved my family dearly and I think they loved me. I repaid them with betrayal.

My particular mind, my particular personality, had led me to a life of intense excitements and 'forbidden-fruits' gain. That particular mind, that particular personality, was totally ungeared for the boredom, the crushing routine of prison life. Some men can switch off their thoughts in jail, let the days go without hearing the tick of a clock. Every tick is an hour apart for me behind bars.

They sent me off to Peterhead prison, thirty miles north of Aberdeen, often known as Scotland's answer to Dartmoor. It is a prison as hard as the granite from which it is built. There are few ways you can rebel in Peterhead, but I found one – a little one, I agree, but it seemed important at the time. Penal servitude meant working in the quarry, wielding a fourteen-pound hammer to break large bits of granite into small bits of granite. The small bits were then carted off for in-filling at an Admiralty harbour scheme nearby. For nearly two years, working under the eyes of warders armed with .303 rifles, I limited my work to the same piece of rock, deliberately slowing the hammer just before impact to avoid shattering it. I trimmed it, I scraped it, I *sculpted* it with as much love as a Michelangelo. In the end, it was an almost perfect sphere. That rock became a talking-point among my fellow prisoners. It even got a name: Paddy's Ball. It must have become too well-known, for someone told the screws.

One day, when I was on a break a few yards away, a warder took my hammer, swung it, and with one blow smashed the ball into a thousand pieces. At the time I was furious – almost in a state of mourning. Then, after a while, I began to think it funny. 'The Screw Who Smashed Paddy's Ball' became a bit of a character round the nick. Now looking back, I realize how ridiculous my obsession with that piece of granite became. What sense is there in a grown man spending a substantial chunk of his life caressing a lifeless rock when, with a bit of sense, he could be caressing his wife's cheeks or his baby's hair? Where's the glamour in that?

4 The springing of Teddy Martin

During that first stretch in Peterhead, I spent more and more time thinking about Peter and his Marxist teachings. I subscribed to the *Daily Worker* and tuned in most days to the Radio Moscow English programmes. Perhaps there was a chance, I thought, of steering my rebelliousness against society into changing that society, for I had come to realize that there was little chance of ever changing myself. I was serious enough to begin studying Russian, a formidable task for someone with little formal education and no one to ask for advice; the problems of Russian grammar were not one of the everyday talking-points of the screws and prisoners at Peterhead.

On my release in 1950, I walked into the Communist Party headquarters in High Street, Glasgow, and became a card carrying member. For several months, I attended a series of meetings and lectures all over the city, many of them in private houses in surprisingly prosperous areas – many teachers, lecturers and other middle-class intellectuals were 'dabbling' at that time. It was before the suppressions of Hungary and Czechoslovakia. The trouble was, they *were* only 'dabblers'. I found the people pleasant and interesting and the speeches stirring, but as for action, it was nonexistent. I quickly surmised, and I have been proved right, that this sort of dilettante Communism would never take a grip on British society. If someone had suggested manning the barricades in a fullscale revolution, I would have been out there flying the Red Flag. I wasn't, however, short of action in my other field of activity.

I had quickly fallen in once again with two villains who were my closest friends. They were the sort of friends who would give you anything they had, and expect the same in return. Friendships like that are not unusual in the underworld. We stick together through thick and thin. Sadly, the thin times can be very thin indeed. Teddy Martin has the sort of Italian looks which drive women wild and a ferocious temper. I met him in Slatefield, where his hatred of the Christian Brothers was matched only by

42

his hatred for the police. Arthur MacTampson is at least as tough and one of the most singleminded men I have ever known. He is happily married, dotes on his children, and never drinks anything stronger than a bottle of beer. He is, however, not a man to cross. Now I have written at length about my views on violence, but it would be foolish to pretend that members of the Glasgow underworld were as pure as the driven snow. Both Teddy and MacTampson were quite capable of cool, extreme violence but, I hasten to add, only within a very strict set of rules. Neither, for instance, would attack an ordinary member of the public, either on a job or in one of the pub brawls which are not an uncommon feature of Glasgow life. Neither would countenance violence towards a woman, or to a man whose womenfolk were present. But they were leading members of a very hard society, and they would protect their position in that society with any force they considered necessary. Other criminals who 'crossed' them did so at their peril. An insult, delivered to them personally, or to a friend would be quickly and forcefully avenged.

In the early fifties, this powder-keg situation existed between Teddy and MacTampson, but nothing happened – yet – to light the fuse. Times were good. I travelled quite extensively, mainly with Teddy, to Dublin, Belfast and Paris. Like all the good times, they weren't to last.

Early in 1953, I was surprised trying to break into an explosives magazine (I will leave the reader to decide why) and it was back to Peterhead for two years. We now had three children. Pat, now six, had been joined by Sally, five and Liz, two; and Betty was becoming increasingly angry. I was soon joined in that granite wilderness by Teddy Martin, who had been convicted of discharging a fire-arm: not to hurt anyone, incidentally, but just as a little warning. One day, we were being marched back from the quarry in silence, when I spoke.

'Who was that?' demanded the screw.

I didn't answer. You don't volunteer information to screws. The warder turned on Teddy, standing next to me, and said: 'All right, Martin, you're going to the cells.'

It was too much for Teddy. Before I could blurt out a 'confession', he stepped forward and landed the warder a straight right. The warder went down like a sack of potatoes and Ted went down for an extra twelve months on his five year sentence. I was filled with guilt, but there was no point by that time in confessing that I had instigated the incident: I would have lost remission too, and that would not have helped Teddy. Before my release, I said to him: 'If you want to go over the wall, I'll fix it.' He just nodded, 'OK'.

No one had ever escaped from Peterhead. To get out of the quarry or the Admiralty yard – where prisoners were working on a breakwater – would not be difficult; but like Dartmoor, Peterhead has formidable hidden walls . . . the wild, open countryside for miles around. A man on foot is a sitting duck. To escape by car is almost as difficult, for there are few roads and a few roadblocks can seal the area tight as a cork in a bottle within an hour.

Back in Glasgow on my release, I discussed the problem with MacTampson. What we needed was a diversion! The problem appealed to MacTampson, who was and is a 'fixer'. I have often thought he should take up chess – he would be a Grand Master in no time. The solution was not long in coming. A prison uniform was smuggled out of Barlinnie jail and Teddy's Peterhead prison number was marked inside the collar.

I was to lead the main attack. At a previously agreed time and place, Teddy was standing by the wall in the Admiralty Yard. A quick leg-up from a fellow prisoner and he was over the wall, dropping down next to the car outside. I was waiting with a civilian suit on the back seat. An excited handshake, a laughing embrace, and we were off, Teddy changing into his new clothes. We drove a few miles, pulled into an hotel and like all good Scotsmen, went for a drink. We saw the squad cars hurtling past, and toasted ourselves in good malt whisky. We knew that back in Glasgow, MacTampson was waiting for a few hours to pass – a realistic time for the journey from Peterhead back to the city – before putting the diversion into operation. It was as simple as that. At the agreed time, MacTampson made an anonymous phone call to the police, saying that a prison uniform had been found in a house in the Black Hill area of Glasgow. The squad cars were there in minutes, followed shortly by a dog team – an unexpected development which nearly brought disaster down upon our heads.

MacTampson, having set up such a splendid scheme, was not a man to miss the fun. He was actually in the house in Black Hill when the squad cars roared up to the door. His plan was to play a bemused visitor, wondering what the hell was going on. He had reckoned without the dog. The house was swarming with bobbies, and within minutes the uniform was brought downstairs. Yes, the number on the collar checked – it was Martin's. MacTampson watched with horror as the outfit was pushed under the nose of the police alsatian. He knew that he had handled the smuggled uniform, but it was too late. Before he could move, the dog spun round on him, growling threateningly. You might be clever enough to fool all the police forces in Scotland, but you'll never fool a dog's nose! It is a remarkable tribute to MacTampson's skill as a fixer that he managed to talk his way out of that one. The dog proved to be the only threat, and it couldn't talk. With the police convinced that Teddy was back in Glasgow, the road-blocks across Scotland were cleared away. Teddy and I had a leisurely meal, drove across some of the finest scenery in Scotland to Fort William, and meandered back to Glasgow via the Bonnie, Bonnie Banks o' Loch Lomond.

The escape caused a major sensation in the Scottish press, and the temperature became unseasonably warm in Glasgow. Teddy and I decided to get out of the heat and took a trip to Ireland. After a couple of weeks we flew to London, but the lure of the old haunts was too much. We returned to Glasgow and the inevitable happened. Someone tipped off the police of our return – we never found out who – and I was back inside.

I drew twelve months for my part in the Peterhead escape, but the CID also wanted to ask some pretty pointed questions about some unorthodox withdrawals which were bothering bank managers in different parts of the country. Bank raids were a fairly new phenomenon in Scotland at that time, for generations of villains had decided that they were 'taboo'. Why that decision was taken, I do not know, because I always thought that if you were going to blow a safe, you might as well blow one where the big money was. Perhaps the older generation thought that banks were 'impossible'. I never liked that word.

I was questioned about a raid on a bank in Oban, where £12,000 disappeared from the safe and another £20,000 in cash and jewellery from deposit boxes – a small fortune in the middle fifties. I was duly charged, but the case was dropped through lack of evidence. The questions about a visit to a bank in the Highlands town of Beauly took a more unfortunate turn, and I drew another six years on top of the twelve months for springing Teddy. I remember the Beauly job with a strange mixture of frustration and humour, for to be honest, it had all the elements of slapstick – a sort of gangster film with custard pies. When we got in, we found to our horror that the bank had no less than five safes. began to blow them, one by one. The first was virtually empty, so was the second. All we had was a few pounds and masses of, to us, worthless documents. The third and the fourth proved the same. How long we could go on blowing safes without being heard was a matter of some anxiety, but I was in that 'grit your teeth, I've come this far and I'm not stopping now' sort of mood. Anyway, there was only the fifth safe left, and that *must* be the jackpot – there was nowhere else in the bank to put the stuff. I had enough gelignite left for the fifth attempt. It was *just* enough. We swung the door open to find . . . another smaller safe inside! Like the characters in some send-up Western, we decided it was time to hit the trail out of town. I always thought the Scottish crown jewels were in Edinburgh, not a small bank in the Highlands. Either that, or the manager was very concerned over the safety of his bottle of sherry for entertaining important customers. Anyway, it was less than funny when I drew a year for each of those safes (including the one that caused us to admit defeat) and I was back in Peterhead. There, everyone was going to make trebly sure that there were to be no more successful escape attempts involving Patrick Connolly Meehan.

Despite the precautions, I did get outside the gates, with .303 bullets whistling round my ears. We were working in the prison yard, where a railway line which connected the yard to the quarry was being dismantled. I was on the back of a lorry supervising the loading of lengths of line, when another prisoner jumped into the cab, started the engine, and roared off at top revs towards the yard gate. We had five or six hundred yards to cover, and in the way stood three guards armed with Lee Enfield service rifles.

The first, with more courage than sense, decided to bar our

way by simply standing in our path. Holding on for grim death as the lorry lurched and bucked over the rough surface, I watched with fascination as the guard's look of determination changed, first to one of indecision and then to one of abject terror as he threw himself sideways with only feet to spare. By this time, the second guard had his rifle to his shoulder and it was time for me to show a little discretion – the better part of valour, we are told. I ducked down behind a pile of railway sleepers as the bullets began to whack past. I could tell by the cracks that a third guard, the one on the gate, had also opened fire. We hit the gate with an immense crash of splintering wood and grinding metal, and we were through. Was this liberty at last, I thought?

Through the gate, we had to slow down to a crawl to make a sharp turn onto the road. As luck would have it, an off-duty screw was walking past. With commendable bravery – I must give him his due – he jumped onto the running board and began wrestling with the driver through the open window. The heavily laden lorry slowed, swerved, mounted the pavement and crashed into a stone dyke. I suppose it took a second or so for me to pick myself up, dust myself down, and decide on my next course of action. My fellow convict, the driver, was disappearing across the fields with several screws on his tail. It was going to be one of the shortest jailbreaks in history. To my right, thirty yards away, stood the main gates of the prison. I jumped down from the back of the lorry, sauntered across with my hands in my pockets and rang the bell.

The astounded face of a screw came into view, spluttering with indignation: 'What the hell are you doing out there, Meehan?'

'I was kidnapped, officer,' I said as I stepped back through the gates I hated so much.

It was the only time in my life I have ever walked back into a jail voluntarily. I had nothing to do with the escape attempt, of course. I was merely a reluctant passenger. The Governor could not disprove the story, and in the end decided to take no action – not even against the man who drove the lorry. Perhaps he wanted to keep it quiet. Paddy Meehan was getting Peterhead a bad name.

I was to do five years in Peterhead, and the lorry escapade was really the only thing I remember with much clarity. I did some more studying, which was of some comfort; but mainly I remember every day being worse than yesterday, the boredom, the frustration, the futility pressing down and down and down.

I was just thirty-three when I was released from Peterhead in 1960. Apart from early childhood, I had spent more time inside approved schools, borstals, and prisons than I had outside. Somewhere along the line, I had been lucky enough to acquire a loving wife and three children who were showing all the signs of growing up to be intelligent and well-adjusted individuals. All that could only be attributed to Betty. My contribution had not been nil – it had been *less* than nil, for my lifestyle actually detracted from Betty's efforts. I can think of no greater self-condemnation.

It was time to find a new life.

Within three weeks of leaving Peterhead, Betty and I flew to Vancouver, leaving the children in the temporary care of my parents. Our plan was to find a permanent base in Canada, lay the foundation of a new and honest life, so that the kids could join us to grow up in a normal home. I swear that I really did try.

I found a job as a welder, but was sacked within weeks because I was not a member of a trade union. I spent a summer as a steward on the Skyline observation coaches of the famous Trans-Canadian Express, one of the world's truly romantic trains. It takes five days to cross the continent through scenery which can only really be described as breathtaking. But it was a seasonable job, dependent on the summer tourists, and when the autumn came I was laid off. I entered into long and expensive negotiations to take over the lease of a restaurant in Vancouver, only to pull out – with high legal costs – when a newly acquired friend, an allegedly 'wily Scot' advised me that the building was due for demolition within a couple of years. I should choose my friends more carefully. I have recently learned that this restaurant is still flourishing. Betty was pregnant again, and the costs of natal care threatened huge bills. Virtually every day letters arrived from the children, demanding to know when the family was to be reunited. The clincher was, as always, money.

There is a time in every criminal's life when he faces the classic dilemma. He wants to get out and 'go straight', to forget the years of the look over the shoulder, the midnight knock on the door. But to get out needs money, and criminals wouldn't be criminals if they knew of ways to earn money legitimately. It is Catch 22 – a man wants to become an honest citizen, but he can only do so by one last act of dishonesty. We call it 'The Get Out' – that last big job which is every criminal's dream, the Big One which will provide enough capital to buy the legitimate business which will keep a man out of nick for the rest of his days. So there I was in Canada, my small reserves of cash running out, no prospects on the horizon, a pregnant wife and a family fretting with loneliness some 5,000 miles away. Perhaps many people could resist it. I couldn't.

Betty flew back to Glasgow, and I followed along by boat using an assumed name. I didn't want the police in Glasgow to know I was home: an alibi of being 5,000 miles away at the time sounds pretty convincing. I docked at Avonmouth and made my way to Glasgow, where Betty and I took a flat in Alexandra Parade. Prospects for the Big One looked good, for the reputation of Glasgow petermen had travelled wide. Within days an emissary from the London underworld was in town. He was looking for men with the nerve and skill to prise open the strongroom of the Westminster Bank at the junction of City Road and Old Street, London, reliably said to contain around a quarter of a million pounds. It was a prestige job, highly suitable for my finale in crime.

It is just another of those terrible ironies that my efforts to break away from crime were to lead directly into the most miserable and sinister period of my life . . .

5 The shooting of Teddy Martin

A major bank robbery is not an escapade to rush into without thought, and on this occasion I had personal reasons for delay. I told our visiting villain from The Smoke, a likeable Cockney called Billy, that I would not undertake the job until Betty had the baby. Billy was far from happy with the delay, but it was take it or leave it as far as I was concerned. Billy decided to take it. This gave us plenty of time to 'case' the bank, so Teddy and I went off to London, hired a car, and began our watch on the building.

Crime, like any other business, needs working capital. The bigger the job, the more capital necessary: hiring cars and living in hotels in central London is not a cheap way of passing the time, and by the time Teddy and I returned to Glasgow, our pockets were considerably lighter. We met Arthur MacTampson in a pub – as he was due to go on the raid and was therefore a 'share-holder' in the deal – Teddy thought it was about time that he met some of the operating expenses.

'We've spent a bloody fortune down there,' said Teddy, a little worse for the drink. 'When are you going to shell out?'

MacTampson was not a man to accuse of being tight with money; in fact, he was not a man to accuse of anything. He slipped his hand in his jacket, produced a wallet, and dropped a £100 note on the counter.

'Will that do you?' he said in a warning tone.

Now anyone who flashed £100 notes around in a pub today would provoke a lot of attention. Back in 1961, when £15 a week was a good wage for a working man, the effect was electrifying – which, no doubt, was exactly what MacTampson wanted. Teddy was far from impressed.

'Are you trying to set us up or something?' he demanded threateningly.

The hairs on the back of my neck began to prickle. These were two men who were, within the criminal fraternity, as tough as anything Glasgow could produce. Within that same fraternity, the greatest insult one man can hurl at another is to suggest that he is trying a 'set-up' – planting evidence that would implicate him in some crime. Teddy was thinking, and probably with some justification, that the £100 was part of the proceeds of crime and, being of such an unusually high denomination, might well have a serial number carefully noted down in some police file. It was eyeball-to-eyeball time. Arthur demanded an apology. Teddy refused. I thought I had saved the situation when I moved in between two glowering men, swept the note off the counter, and counted £100 of my own money into Teddy's palm. I was wrong...

It was around one AM Saturday 25th March 1961, that Arthur pulled the trigger on Teddy. The shooting – since it took place in my flat – created problems for me. My immediate problem was to persuade Arthur not to pull the trigger again, not to take Teddy piggy-back (give him a 'coaxy', as they say in Glasgow) down to the thirty hundredweight van parked in the street below. Arthur isn't the type to leave a corpse lying around; he's the tidy sort. But it was Betty who saved the day. On hearing the shot she came through from the bedroom.

'What was that bang?' she asked as she entered the living room. And when she saw the crimson stain spread across the front of Teddy's shirt, she screamed: 'My God, Teddy, what happened to you!'

'He fell,' said Arthur, slipping the gun into his raincoat pocket. Villain though he be, it wasn't Arthur's style to misbehave in the presence of a woman. 'You've got a lot to thank Betty for,' Arthur told Teddy. 'If she hadn't been here, I'd have taken you away.' Then, turning to me, he said, 'Sorry this happened in your flat, Paddy.'

I too was sorry that it had happened in my flat and when Arthur took his leave I breathed a sigh of relief: I had a few sighs of relief to breathe before that night was through. I sat Teddy on the sofa and had a quick look at the damage. The bullet had hit high up in his left shoulder and exited in the small of his back. It looked bad and I wondered if I might have to get Arthur to come back and give Teddy a wee coaxy after all. There was a lot of blood and the sight of it sent Betty near to hysterics. But Teddy was taking it well.

'Look in the top pocket of my jacket and see if the bullet broke my reading glasses,' he said, his tone contemptuous. He had guts. I took hold of Betty and sat her on the sofa.

'Now listen very carefully,' I told them both, 'this is the story.' When I finished telling them the story – it would help the police, if we all told the same story! – I hurried from the flat.

In the street below, Arthur's van was parked opposite, with Arthur behind the wheel. Some fifty yards away was a phone box. As I made towards it, the van became mobile, went into a U-turn, and drew alongside me. The nearside door slid open. I went forward and leaned in.

'Sure you don't want me to take him off your hands?' said MacTampson.

'Quite sure,' I told him. 'You make yourself scarce and get rid of the artillery. I'll be in touch later.'

'What about a story?' said MacTampson. 'You'll need a good one.'

'That's been taken care of,' I said.

'Sorry it happened the way it did,' said MacTampson. 'I didn't plan to shoot him in your flat. And anyway, why didn't he back down? I gave him the chance to back down, why didn't he take it?'

'Because he's like you,' I said, 'stark raving mad.'

MacTampson gave out a loud laugh. I slammed the van door to and hurried towards the phone box. As the van passed me I could hear MacTampson's laugh above the noise of the engine.

Vandals had been at work. The phone box was in darkness. I had to peer hard to find the nine. I found it and dialled three times. A man's voice came on the line. 'Emergency. Can I help you?'

'Ambulance,' I said. 'And make it quick.'

'What's your number?'

'What?'

'Your number! What number are you calling from?'

I peered hard at the disc, but the light was too poor to make out the digits. 'I can't see the number. There's no light in this box.'

'Sorry, I can't put you through without the number. I must have the number.' I couldn't believe my ears.

'Put me through, you bloody idiot!' I screamed. 'A man's been shot, might be dying . . .'

'Haven't you got a match?'

'What?'

'A match. Strike a match, then you'll see the number. I'm sorry but I . . .'

At that moment there was the sound of an engine. I turned. Through the glass door I could see a vehicle approaching. It was a taxi, its FOR HIRE sign illuminated. I shot out of the box waving my arms wildly. The taxi slowed to a stop. The driver stuck his head out.

'Can you do a hospital job, Mac?' I asked.

'Maternity?' asked the driver.

'No.' I said. 'Not maternity. It's a friend of mine. He's been hurt.'

'Sure,' said the driver.

'Can you come up and help me get him down? He's in my flat.'

The driver started to get out. 'Sure,' he said. 'What's wrong with him?'

I tried to sound off-hand. 'He's been shot.'

'He's been what?' said the driver, getting back into the cab.

'He's in a bad state Mac. Might be dying.' My tone was urgent. I had to get the driver to come up to the flat. He'd be an independent witness to anything said by Teddy. And, if Teddy died, I'd need an independent witness badly.

'I'm not allowed to touch that kind of job,' said the driver, 'but if you give me the details I'll have an ambulance here in a jiffy.' I gave him the address. He put this out on his two-way radio. 'Ambulance will be here in no time,' he said, when he finished relaying the information. But I still had to get him up to the flat.

'Maybe you can help save his life. You know, first aid or something.'

'Well, I do know a little about first aid,' he said, and got out.

I sensed he was the decent type, ready to help in an emergency. We started walking towards the flats; then he stopped as if something had occurred to him.

53

'Who's up there?'

'My wife,' I told him.

'What about . . . you know . . . the other chap?' He was a cautious taxi driver.

'You mean the fellow who shot him! He's not there. He didn't stay long. My wife and kids are in the flat.'

When we got up to the flat Teddy was still sprawled on the living room sofa. He was still conscious but didn't look too healthy. Betty was at the window, from where she had been giving Teddy a running commentary on what was going on in the street below. She had seen me stop the taxi. When I told her we'd have to wait for the ambulance she became agitated. While I was pacifying her the taxi driver had a look at Teddy.

'There's not much I can do for that one. Who did it, mate?'

'I don't know,' Teddy replied. 'He was wearing a mask.'

The taxi driver looked at me, uncertain.

'That's right,' I said. 'Big fellow. Six foot two. Had a cockney accent.' I looked at Teddy for confirmation.

'One of the London mob,' said Teddy.

'Don't talk so much, Teddy,' said Betty from the window. 'Try to save your strength.' That was just like Betty. I want Teddy to talk as much as possible; and she tells him to keep quiet.

'What about a drink?' I asked the taxi driver. 'Would you like a drop of the hard stuff?'

'I could do with some of that too,' said Teddy.

'Sure,' said the driver. 'But just a nip.'

'My God! What's keeping the ambulance?' said Betty. She was near to tears. I got a bottle of whisky from the cabinet and began to pour. 'There's a couple of uniformed policemen down there,' she said. 'I think they are coming up.'

No sooner had she spoken than there was a terrific clatter on the outside stairway. I had left the front door wide open to allow the ambulance men to walk straight in. Suddenly, two heavily breathing policemen came barging into the living room. One of them, the larger of the two, knew Teddy.

'Oh, it's you Teddy.' The notebooks came out. 'Who did it, Teddy?'

'I don't know who did it,' said Teddy.

'That's right,' I said. 'A big fellow, he was, wore a mask and spoke with a cockney accent. About six foot two and . . .'

The large constable glowered at me. 'Who are you?' he asked.

'Mr Carson.' I told him, using my assumed name. 'This is my flat.' As I spoke I lifted the taxi driver's nip and downed it.

'And who are you?' said the large constable, turning his glare on the taxi driver.

The taxi driver moved back from the table as if to indicate that he wasn't one of the family. Then he began to explain his presence in the flat. As he was talking there was the sound of activity in the street below.

'That's the ambulance now,' said Betty. 'And there's a couple of cars there too.'

'That will be the CID,' said the large constable.

I picked up another whisky, and downed it. It was the CID all right. Five or six of them led by a detective called McDougall, no stranger to me. The large constable pointed to me. 'This is Mr Carson, the owner of the flat.'

'Mr Carson, my arse,' said McDougall. 'That's Paddy Meehan. Get him against the wall and search him.' Two detectives crowded me and backed me against the wall.

'He's got nothing to do with it!' Betty screamed.

The ambulance men placed the stretcher on the floor and prepared to lift Teddy onto it. Teddy got to his feet. 'I'll walk,' he said, and staggered out of the flat supported by one of the ambulance men. The detectives finished searching me.

'Get him down to the station,' McDougall told them.

I suppose you could hardly blame them, under the circumstances. Here was a known Glasgow villain with a .38 bullet hole in him. Found on the scene was another known villain, living under an assumed name. I would have thought I had done the shooting if I had been in their shoes! If Teddy were to die – and I had no reason to know that he wouldn't – there was a very real danger that I would be convicted of the murder. The police played on this fear while they cross-examined me. Every thirty minutes or so, a detective would lift the phone, carefully within my hearing, and ask: 'What's the latest on Martin?' The voice at the other end would reply: 'No change – he's still in a coma.'

Later that night, McDougall rolled his eyes to the ceiling and said: 'Are you asking me to believe that a man wearing a mask just walked in through an open door, shot Martin, and walked out again without you doing anything about it?'

'I can only tell you what happened,' I said.

'But why didn't you tackle him?'

'You must be joking. He was about 6 feet 2 inches, but it would have made no difference if he was 2 feet 6 – he had a bloody great service Webley.'

And so it went on. The questioning strayed from the shooting to my trip to Vancouver. There were also questions about a bank job in the North of England, where something like £40,000 disappeared. It came as something of a surprise when McDougall finally said: 'I'm letting you go. I know you didn't shoot Martin, but you know who did. Perhaps one day you'll tell me.'

Outside the police station, I telephoned the hospital and learned that Teddy, although he had undergone an operation, was not in a coma. He always had been a tough so-and-so. That night, I blessed the strength of his constitution.

6 Hector, Sheila

The police were not the only people whose interests were aroused by the shooting of Teddy Martin. And the repercussions from MacTampson's £100 note were only just beginning. The following day, I went to visit Teddy in hospital. He was as cheerful and unrepentant as ever. When I said I intended to call off the London bank job, he was amazed.

'Don't be bloody ridiculous,' he said. 'Betty's still got to have the baby, and I'll be fighting fit in a week's time. This job's too good to be missed for a little thing like this . . .'

A nurse was hovering close by, making it difficult to talk, but if Teddy had decided that a .38 bullet was only a little thing, who was I to contradict him?

'Is there anything I can get you?' I asked loudly for the nurse's benefit.

He pulled down the bedclothes and displayed the regulation flannel nightdress he was wearing. 'Would you buy me some pyjamas?' he grinned. 'I feel a right poof in this lot.'

I nodded: 'I'll have to go to the GPO and change this bloody note – the £100 is all I've got on me.'

Off I went. As I came out of the main post office in George Square, I noticed a man 'hovering' on the pavement. I say hovering because he was obviously interested in me, but seemed diffident about making an approach. A man in my trade is used to that sort of attention, but this fellow, standing about five-feet-nine in a well-cut herringbone coat, was no detective I knew. After a few seconds, he came towards me, snapping his fingers.

'It's Paddy isn't it?' he asked speculatively. 'Paddy . . . Paddy . . . eh . . . ?'

I have little time for these polite social games when you have forgotten someone's name. In this case, I was quite convinced that this guy really was playing: he knew fine well who I was.

'Paddy Meehan,' I said curtly, and moved as if to walk past him. He moved into my path and said gently but with some firmness: 'You have obviously forgotten me, but we met before at one of the meetings. I am a friend of Peter's.'

At the mention of Peter's name, my interest perked up. Although I had long stopped any active participation in Communist Party affairs, I still had a great sympathy for the cause. Peter was a man I remembered with great affection – I have already said he was one of the most genuine men I have ever met – and he was one of the very few people with whom I had maintained a correspondence over the years.

'Perhaps we could have a little talk?' the stranger asked. I explained I had some shopping to do, and that I was driving back to the hospital.

'That's lucky, I'm going that way myself,' he said in his educated Glasgow accent. 'Perhaps you would give me a lift?'

During the short drive, his questions began to get more and more pointed. I was being 'pumped' and I knew it, but did not object . . . the world I lived in was full of people who deemed it necessary to make roundabout approaches. Sometimes these approaches could lead to considerable profit.

'Peter and I talk about you a lot,' he confided. 'You wrote to him from prison once upon a time, didn't you?'

'That's right,' I said casually, but it had been 'once upon a time' – three years previously, to be more precise.

'And was this Teddy Martin who was shot last night the same man you sprang from Peterhead?'

'That's right,' I said again. He was getting somewhere near the point. If he were a copper, I thought, he already knew that anyway – but his approach was a good deal more subtle than anything I had experienced before.

'I see some comrades are in serious trouble,' he said, and opened a newspaper he produced from his pocket.

'Do you think you could do anything for them?'

We had arrived at the hospital, so I stopped the car and took the paper. The page carried banner headlines about the Portland Spy Case, and the Krogers, that had just ended in London. The case – involving the infamous Gordon Lonsdale and the Krogers, a team of professional Russian spies, and Harry Houghton, the Royal Navy man who had passed over some of the world's most advanced information about submarine detection equipment – had caused a sensation throughout the Western world. The same page also carried a report of the shooting of Teddy Martin.

'I bet you couldn't spring one of those spies,' challenged the stranger. 'They'll be watching them like hawks.'

It was put in an ordinary conversational tone, a throw-away comment on a situation which was only a matter of passing interest. Despite the tone, this was a definite 'feeler'.

I thought for about ten seconds, before answering with some emphasis: 'Given the proper organization and back-up, I could spring anyone from any jail in Britain.'

We each turned to stare into the other's face. He still wore an expression of bland curiosity, but his eyes were as hard as steel.

'Do you really think you could do it?'

'I've just told you so, haven't I?'

I was, by now, thoroughly interested, but he would not drop the 'idle curiosity' approach. He began every question with, 'I should think...'

'I should think the Russians would pay well to have one of their top men sprung...'

'I should think you should have a good long talk with them...'

That shouldn't be difficult, I volunteered. All I had to do was to pop into the Russian Embassy in London and have a chat. That was the nearest he ever came to showing any real emotion. He gave just the slightest suggestion of a shudder.

'Oh I wouldn't think they'd like that,' he said. 'I think if you really wanted to demonstrate your good faith, you'd go somewhere behind the Iron Curtain – East Berlin would be a good place, wouldn't you say? – just to show that you mean real business.'

'I suppose I could have a talk with a couple of friends of mine,' he added mysteriously. 'Perhaps we could meet again in a couple of days?'

I agreed, and we arranged time and place. As he stepped from the car I leant forward and called after him: 'What should I call you, by the way?'

He smiled: 'I don't think we need go into that. You'll think of something, no doubt...'

'Alright, I'll call you Hector,' I said.

He smiled and hurried away. He could not know that Hector was a joke name in my life . . . I had used it for many accomplices while on jobs. Criminals (as we will hear later) do not use their real names while working, just in case there is anyone within earshot. Names are good evidence – sometimes!

We had our meeting two days later, where his questions were a little more pragmatic: was my passport up to date? Had any of my friends served time in English jails? Where could he get in touch with me in the near future? I told him I was off to London 'on a little business' – I didn't say what – and gave him a number to ring. It was the number of Billy's flat in Hackney. As he left the car the second time – he had only agreed to sit in the car, he wouldn't meet me in a pub – he smiled his enigmatic smile and said: 'Try and keep out of trouble in the next few weeks.'

It was the last time I was ever to see him. But I was to hear from him in even more mysterious circumstances.

On April 1st, 1961 – he was to be no fool, despite his birthday – Gary Meehan came into the world, our fourth and final child. I had promised to stay by Betty's side until after the birth. This promise honoured, I was free to travel to London for the Great Westminster Bank bonanza – the Big One which was to pay for the new life Betty and I were planning for our burgeoning family, this time in Australia.

Teddy and I booked into an hotel, but were persuaded after a few days to move to a house in Balham, southwest London. The persuasion came from Billy, who introduced us to the householder, a shapely and stylish brunette called Sheila. Sheila's husband, we were told, was serving a three year jail sentence, the sort of 'reference' which, in our topsy-turvy world, villains like from their prospective landlady. Landladies can see and hear too much. Comings and goings in the night seem unusual to straight citizens. Sheila didn't pose these threats. And anyway, she was pretty. But the disasters started almost immediately. Teddy and Joe – a Glasgow villain shipped in to replace MacTampson after the shooting – were caught red-handed in the Westminster Bank when the police walked in. A man working late in a nearby office had heard the explosion. Yet again, the Big One had slipped my grasp.

With my new-found London contacts, I began to look around for another target. There was one bank which looked particularly promising, but it would need several weeks of casing before any attempt could be made. The wait was becoming too much for Billy, who had already been sitting on his hands since his first approach to me in Glasgow weeks before. He lined up a nearby Co-op store, whose weekend takings were said to tot up to a reasonably tasty £8,000. Would I go? My answer was a direct No. There were too many men involved in the job, making the share-out unworthy of the risk. I would rather wait around for the new bank.

Two weekends running, Billy pressed me to go on the Co-op caper. Twice I refused. On the third weekend, I was sitting in Sheila's house watching 'Candid Camera' on the television when Billy came round yet again. He was very agitated.

'You've got to come, Paddy,' he begged. 'We've made the break, the safe is already primed – all you have to do is set it off.'

'In that case, you don't need me,' I grumbled.

Billy was shame-faced: 'Well, we do Paddy – you see, none of us have ever done a safe before!'

At this, Sheila joined in, bringing the full weight of her un-doubted charms to bear. 'If you don't do it for them, do it for me,' she vamped suggestively. 'Go on – they need a pro. I'll drive you there myself. You'll be in and out in two minutes.'

I had, after all, been living in her house, and Billy, after all, had put himself to a great deal of effort on my behalf. The com-bined pressure was too much; reluctantly, I pulled on a pair of gloves, although I didn't bother to change out of my cardigan and carpet slippers. My reluctance turned to horror when, within half an hour, I was standing over two safes in the Co-op's cashier's booth. God help me, I thought, I've wound up with a bunch of amateurs. The safes were packed to overflowing with gelignite.

'The Dam-Busters used less than this to flood half Germany,' I commented savagely, and began picking bits of gelignite *out* of the locks. That's what I was doing when the cops walked in – taking gelignite out of a safe. I was to use that to back up my 'Not Guilty' plea at the Old Bailey, the most famous court in the world, a month later. The jury didn't see the joke. I was using my alias

61

of Carson, but a fingerprint check had inevitably brought my record roaring down from Scotland. I drew eight years PD – Preventative Detention, the formal acknowledgement from the English legal system that you are a professional criminal. You are detained, not in the hope of reforming your soul, but to *prevent* you practising your trade to the further detriment of straight society.

Thinking is the one exercise that a man can practise to his heart's content in the nick. Walls, bars, locks, screws and oppressive routine cannot stop a man's mind turning over. I was stuck in London's Wandsworth prison, and I did a lot of thinking. There had been just two jobs in London, and two disasters. Scotland Yard may have the finest detectives in the world, but my friends in crime were hardly amateurs. A 100 percent success rate for the Yard was just too good to be true. There are arrests which every criminal accepts as being part of the luck of the draw. Perhaps he has made a stupid mistake, leaving vital evidence behind – fingerprints, perhaps, or a piece of traceable equipment. That's his own fault.

A lucky cop might stop you in your car or on the street, your boot or pockets bulging with loot. If you weren't speeding in the car – stupidity if you are carrying booty – or carrying a heavy bag in the early hours of the morning – even greater stupidity – the 'accidental' arrest is sheer misfortune. But to be disturbed in the commission of a crime is an event which turns the criminal mind to the question: was there a tip-off? When the cops walk in on two successive jobs, the question becomes: who gave the tip-off? In other words, *who grassed*?

It couldn't have been Teddy, for obvious reasons. Apart from my absolute trust in his loyalty, he was already inside when the second arrest was made. Billy was a better possibility, but he had drawn five years for the Co-op job. So that ruled him out. My mind turned to the question posed in the detective stories: *cherchez la femme*. The dark and beautiful Sheila, the woman who had applied every ounce of charm to make me go to the Co-op that night. Sheila; it was the logical answer. But the unanswerable question was: Why? I couldn't believe she would have done such a thing for a few back-hand quid from the Yard

– she wasn't the sort to be that short of cash. No, I decided it could not have been Sheila. Perhaps it had been bad luck after all. So I put the matter out of my mind. I have watched too many men drive themselves to the point of madness trying to answer the question: Who betrayed me?

The Old Bailey sentence had been too much for Betty. The record told my life story: seven years in approved schools, and the number of jail sentences had passed the 21 mark. She threw in the towel, and started separation proceedings. This was as big a blow as life had ever handed me, much more severe than Mr Justice Maud's eight years at the Old Bailey. If I had ever had any intention of serving out the full sentence in English jails, it left me with the thought of losing Betty. And anyway, my horizons had widened. One of the most important documents I ever read was also one of the shortest. It arrived, quite normally, through the post at Wandsworth. The postcard said simply: 'Sorry to hear about your troubles. Regards, Hector.'

How did Hector know I was in Wandsworth? After all, the English papers which had covered the trial – and there was little interest – had used my alias of Carson. I had no reason to believe that such a minor case had made the Scottish papers. I assumed that Hector must have made contact with Betty, an assumption which I couldn't check because, for fairly obvious reasons, Betty and I were not corresponding at the time. The postcard finally convinced me, if I still had any doubts, that Hector was a Communist agent. In that case, the card could only mean one thing: we are still interested! Suddenly, this Scottish peterman in an English jail felt the world was at his feet. Betty and I had planned for Australia, with its Commonwealth links and its simple extradition laws. If I could get the KGB as my travel agents, anywhere was possible: Brazil, America, literally anywhere, with cast-iron papers and plenty of money in the bank. All I had to do in return was to deliver them one of their top spies! Billy and I threw ourselves into escape plots with an unprecedented zeal.

First we turned to Johnny the Bosch, one of the star characters of the English underworld, one of the greatest key-smiths ever. John could watch a screw put a key in a lock and, with his photographic memory, go away and a few days later run up a duplicate in the prison workshop. He was not always spot on: he always made three slightly different duplicates. One invariably worked.

Johnny had been moved out of Wandsworth, leaving behind his collection of valuable keys. One day, Billy arranged for another prisoner – a cleaner – to unlock his cell and come creeping downstairs to release me. But a screw had stationed himself at my door making it impossible for Billy to unlock me. As agreed beforehand, Billy had to go it alone. He got over the wall, stripped off down to his pants and prison vest – which now sported a sewed-on Number Nine. He set off through the streets of London like a dedicated harrier, rounded a corner, and ran straight into the arms of an off-duty screw. Recognition was instantaneous: Billy was back inside within minutes and for his trouble lost 180 days remission and was shipped off to the Special Unit at Durham prison.

It was back to the drawing board for me – an operation which was not too difficult because, puzzlingly, I was still classed as an ordinary-class prisoner. I assumed my escape record in Scotland had not filtered down to London, for otherwise I would surely have been in the 'High Risk' security class. After fourteen months, this puzzle deepened. I was due for transfer, under the PD system, to another high-security prison for the remainder of my sentence. I had expected it to be Parkhurst on the Isle of Wight, a very tough nick surrounded by a lot of sea. Few escape from Parkhurst. My delight at discovering that, instead, I was to be sent to Nottingham jail, can be readily understood. If I were to be of real assistance to the KGB, I realized that I could not escape alone: I would have to recruit at least one prisoner, and perhaps more, who had detailed knowledge of many English prisons. I knew many of the tricks useful to a wouldbe escaper – how to smuggle in equipment, how to enlist the assistance of bent screws, how to organize the get-away – which would work at any prison. But to 'sell' my plan to the KGB – I had no doubts that this would be an incredibly difficult task – I needed inside plans of jails where Russian spies were likely to be held. At Nottingham, I chose 'Sonny', a man who had served several sentences and was familiar with Wormwood Scrubs, London, and Birmingham's Winson Green. Sonny was to be a bad choice.

The next move was to get my hands on some hacksaw blades. This did not involve my dear old mother baking me a cake with a steel centre – nothing so romantic. MacTampson simply paid someone to walk up to the jail walls one dark night and toss the blades over the wall into a little used corner of the yard, wrapped in a dirty old cloth. I then paid one of the prison cleaners to retrieve the innocent looking piece of rubbish. For months, we worked on the bars of a cell that was being used as a card room. The opportunities to work uninterrupted were few and far between. It is hard, tedious work, rough on the hands and even rougher on the mind, living in constant fear of interruption, dreading every cell search by screws who might notice the marks on the bars, which were disguised with breadcrumbs mixed with dust, a cover which would only have survived the most casual inspection. Fortunately, casual the inspections were.

On the freezing cold, snowy evening of Boxing Day 1962, Sonny, myself and three fellow prisoners finally pulled away the bars and made our way into the prison yard. We had anticipated discovery, and it came from one of the 'good screws', Mr Overton, who walked straight into us. I took him by the arm and said, gently, but firmly: 'We don't mean you any harm, but we want to go home. If you've any sense, you won't resist.'

Outnumbered five to one, he didn't. We bound him as planned – I had insisted all along that no harm was to be done to any of the prison staff. I had not bargained for Sonny's reaction. The sight of the 'screw' bound and helpless was too much for him.

'Let's do him over – let's put the boot in,' he whispered in a state of high excitement. Too late I realized he had a strong sadistic streak. 'They'll give us plenty of stick just for tying him up,' he went on, 'so we might as well go the whole hog.'

I stepped between them, shaking with rage. I waved a fist underneath Sonny's nose and snarled: 'Lay a finger on him and I'll go the whole hog on you.' Like many cruel men, Sonny was a coward. He backed down.

We struggled to climb the wall with the ropes we had 'acquired', but the top was covered in frozen snow. I remember my fingernails biting into the ice as I slipped cursing back into the yard. I hit the ground and the alarm went off simultaneously. It was back to the cells. Later, Overton came in and stuttered bashfully: 'Look Meehan, this is a difficult thing for me to say ... but thank you for what you did out in the yard. That bastard would have half killed me just for the laughs ...'

'Forget it,' I cut him short. I was more embarrassed than he was, a *screw* covering me with *praise*. It was unheard of.

As I was ringleader of the escape attempt, the visiting Magistrates – local JPs who impose prison discipline for more serious offences – lopped 180 days off my remission, gave me nine days on bread and water and 28 in solitary. More seriously, they recommended my transfer to the Special Unit at Durham jail, the nearest thing England has to Colditz Castle (and later to be the home of some of the Great Train Robbers, amongst many others). This was a real blow. Even my boundless optimism slumped as I weighed up the odds of escaping from Durham.

It was in a state of deep depression that, my solitary in Nottingham served out, I changed into civilian clothes for the transfer. My best chance, I was thinking, would be to make a break on the journey. To expect half a chance was too much: I was to have an escort of three men. But if a quarter chance came along I would have to take it.

Then a decision was made which to me, at the time, was completely inexplicable – the transfer was cancelled at the very last second. Why? I asked. 'The Home Office say you should stay here.' Nevertheless, I remained at Nottingham as a Category 'A' prisoner, the top security risk, and wore large white patches on my prison uniform, front and back. My clothing was taken from my cell every evening and I was forced to sleep with a light blazing overhead all night. During the day, I was accompanied at all times by two warders one of whom – a dash of slapstick I thought – carried a photograph of me; presumably to ensure that I had not switched personalities. But I doubt if there were any screws in that jail who didn't have the face of Paddy Meehan burned into their brains. I gave them the normal couple of months to drop their guard: no human being can keep his wits on total alert for much longer than that, particularly under the numbing boredom of prison routine, which is as bad for the staff as it is for their charges. Then I contacted MacTampson again: more hacksaw blades, please!

I had also collected two more experts on the English prison

system, Paddy, one of the few men ever to make a successful break from Parkhurst on the Isle of Wight, and a Londoner called Joe, an 'old boy' of so many nicks that he could recite them with all the relish of a ne'er-do-well public schoolboy who has been expelled from every boarding school in the country. We were almost halfway through the bars of a storeroom window – the result of a minute's work here, a minute's work there, over a period of weeks – when Governor Footer called for me. Mr Footer, a former Army officer, told me that I had been removed from the Category 'A' list and restored to the rank of ordinary prisoner. Even he looked puzzled. I was amazed, and not at all pleased – both Paddy and Joe were Category 'A' men, and this meant separation from them for most of the time, making our plans even more of a challenge. No one in Nottingham prison could understand my 'demotion', staff or prisoners. Eventually, everyone assumed that someone in Whitehall had made a typing error – these things do happen from time to time. The slow process of sawing through the storeroom bars went on and on. Three months later, Governor Footer called for me again. I was to be made a 'Red Band' – a trusty allowed to work *outside* the prison walls *without escort*! In other words, I was being thrown out onto the streets of Nottingham, able to wave down the first passing cab and jump onto the first train to Glasgow or London – and thence the first plane to Berlin! My demotion from Category 'A' had been a shock. This latest news stupefied me. What the hell was going on!

Screws and prisoners alike took to shaking their heads with amazement every time they saw me. My red arm band – symbol of the trusty – went onto the uniform where the discoloured patches left by the white Category 'A' markers could still be seen. It was almost as if they were inviting me to escape. There was only one conclusion I could reach: the Governor had taken leave of his senses?

It was only a matter of days, of course, before MacTampson took a train from Glasgow to Nottingham. We met each other in a welter of mutual astonishment. He had a little present for me, the sort of gadget every high-class prisoner should own, a pair of heavy-duty wire cutters. For although I could have gone back to Glasgow with MacTampson that day, I still had the problem of 'collateral' for the KGB – the intimate knowledge of the English prison system stored in the heads of Paddy and Joe. I remember muttering to myself, in a state of childish joy, that typically upper-class phrase, 'This really isn't cricket, old boy,' as I laid the plans for our latest and – because of my new found trusty status – simpler escape plan. Paddy and Joe were to get out through the wire of the exercise field during a prison cricket match one afternoon in June 1963.

As it happened, Paddy couldn't get to the game. But Joe sheared through the security fence in seconds. We went to the car and were away. It must have been the simplest escape in English prison history.

We spent the night in Sherwood Forest – guarded by the ghost of Robin Hood, no doubt – our car heavily camouflaged with foliage. Next morning we drove to London, where Joe took me to a house in Islington. To my surprise, the householders turned out to be relatives of the raven-haired Sheila. What a coincidence! Then Joe said quite casually that he had known Sheila from way back. London is one of the biggest cities in the world, but I seemed to have turned it into a village.

'Would you like to see her?' someone asked.

'Why not?' I said.

A youngster, who was a friend of Joe's, went off to fetch her, but returned soon afterwards with the message: 'She's away in Spain.'

I had no time to worry about Sheila. It was a time of hectic comings and goings, of people picking up my passport for me (it had been left at a house in Nottingham, but I had decided not to risk picking it up), of travelling to Glasgow and back. I needed to go to Glasgow to contact Hector. I was sure he would have been in touch with Betty, for the Scottish papers were full of my escape. No, said Betty, there had been no word. I was in a dilemma. My reasons for escaping had been implanted by Hector's postcard to Wandsworth. I had with me Joe, whose knowledge was as valuable as mine from the Communist point of view. And I obviously could not stay in Glasgow – I was too well known. So, telling Joe to wait in Glasgow – 'I don't know how long it will be, but a couple of weeks at the most' – I returned to London.

There, I heard a worrying story. A woman friend had driven

down from Edinburgh to Nottingham to pick up my passport. From Nottingham, she drove on to London and noticed, after some miles, that she was apparently being 'tailed' by an unmarked car. It followed them all the way to London, right to an address in Dalston which was one of our 'safe' houses – she had more sense than to take them anywhere near a place where someone was actually hiding. After she entered the house, it was surrounded by police and searched. They took nothing away and gave the occupants no idea of what they were searching for. But the men who had been in the 'tail' car from Nottingham introduced themselves as Scotland Yard officers. Now what was a Scotland Yard car doing 100 miles away from its manor? We pondered it but gave up: there was no obvious conclusion we could reach, and I, in particular, had other things to worry about. Was my passport a 'marked' document? If so, every emigration official and Customs man in the land would have its number, along with a picture and detailed description of me. I decided to get another one – a decision which was to lead me into another of those slapstick comedy routines which seem to make a mockery of even the tensest moments of my life. There I was in the passport office in London's Petty France, armed with a false birth-certificate in the name of Martin Dunlievy, and my two photographs signed, falsely, by a friend describing himself as a civil servant. The young clerk looked at me suspiciously.

'The man who gave these references says he is a civil servant?' he asked.

'That's right,' I answered glibly.

'Is he a very good one?' asked the youth.

'Oh yes,' I said, 'a very senior one – he's a very important fellow.'

'That's odd,' said the youth. 'I didn't think a man in a senior position would spell servant with a c.'

There it was on the form, civil *cervant*. I suddenly remembered a very urgent phone call.

As you don't need passports to enter the Irish Republic, I took the next plane to Dublin. My next stop was the Hotel Carlton in Frankfurt am Main, West Germany. Joe was waiting patiently in Glasgow.

7 Behind the curtain

Next morning I booked out of the Hotel Carlton and crossed the street to the station where I bought a return ticket to West Berlin. Then I made a startling discovery; the wallet containing my passport was gone. I could recall having the wallet in the hotel bedroom before I retired the previous night. I returned to the hotel room, made a thorough search, but failed to find it. I enquired at the reception desk, but no wallet had been handed in there. Now what! I decided to take a chance on getting to West Berlin without my passport. I returned to the station and boarded the train.

About fifteen minutes before the train would cross into East Germany, the compartment door slid open and a uniformed official entered. He spoke to me in German but I shrugged my shoulders to indicate that I did not understand. A young woman sitting opposite came to his assistance.

'He wishes to see your passport,' she said in English.

I made a pretence of searching my pockets and then my hold-all. Then I gave up.

'Tell him I seem to have lost my passport,' I told the young woman.

'He says you cannot travel through the Zone without your passport,' said the young woman. 'It is very dangerous. The Communists will arrest you and put you in prison. He says you must leave the train at the next stop.'

The next stop, the last before the Border, was a place called Badhersfeld. I left the train and booked in at a nearby hotel, Hotel Kaiserhof. I booked a room for three days. I reckoned I'd have some reconnoitring to do. By road, Badhersfeld lies some fifteen kilometres from the East German border, as I learned from a salesgirl who sold me a German/English dictionary.

'But no buses go that way,' the girl told me. 'It's a dead end.'

A bicycle seemed to be the answer. A young boy sold me one for fifty marks. It was held together by bits of string and I knew I hadn't got myself a bargain. The boy obviously knew this too;

as soon as I handed him the fifty-mark note, he ran like hell.

Early next morning I got up, paid for the room for a further three days and, leaving my holdall behind, set out for the Border. In that part of Germany there are many hills; and all of them go up – never down. I pedalled on blinded by sweat and I was relieved when the high watchtowers of the East German border came into view.

There it was. But how was I going to get across without getting myself shot? I got close up to the border. Close enough to have a clear view of the guards on the nearest watchtower. One of the guards was using binoculars which were pointed in my direction. In the field below the watchtower a number of farm workers, men and women, were at work. The sight reminded me of a prison work party. I decided I didn't like that spot. I'd move along, parallel to the border and try to find a spot where I'd be out of sight of any watchtower. But I found no such spot.

After cycling along a disused farm track for miles I could see watchtowers looming up ahead. By this time the sun was high and I decided to do a little sunbathing while I thought things over. I particularly wanted to think, because sign boards were spaced out at intervals along the border. They were in German and the thought occurred to me that they just might be 'mine warning' signs. I found myself a suitable spot on a rise overlooking the border and stretched out to enjoy the warm sunshine. I didn't enjoy it for long. I was just dropping into a state of happy tranquillity when near at hand there was the sound of animal grunting. I didn't take time to figure out what it might be. I shot to my feet like a jack-in-the-box. There, a few yards from me, stood a large Dobermann pinscher, saliva dripping from its jaws. It looked big enough to eat me. I stood perfectly still, not by deliberate choice; but because I was terror stricken.

'Christ,' I thought, 'if that thing attacks me I'll be over that border fence double quick, land mines or no.'

The Dobermann stretched its front paws, lowered its head then sprang sideways. It wanted to play. Was I glad! Then I saw it had a small rubber ball in its mouth. I looked around for a sight of anyone who might be with the dog. There was no one in sight. The dog dropped the ball and moved back invitingly. I picked up the ball and threw it as far as I could. The dog bounded after it.

I jumped on the bike and pedalled back the way I had come as fast as my legs would whirl. But the Dobermann wasn't finished with me yet. I hadn't pedalled very far when I heard its heavy grunts coming up behind. I stopped and got off the bike. Again I picked up the ball, but this time I threw it as hard as I could right over the border fence into East German territory. The dog bounded forward then – as if it had had second thoughts – slid to a stop. It turned and looked at me as if to ask: 'What kind of an idiot do you take me for?' Then it trotted off in the direction it had come. I am sure that Dobermann pinscher could read.

I stayed on the bike until I reached a large village, where I had a meal in a small restaurant. The sun was well down as I cycled out of the village towards a river that ran in the direction of the border. I followed a footpath and soon came to a spot where the ruins of a steel bridge lay in the river. About 200 yards away was a watchtower. The guards were looking in my direction. I went right up to where the border fence met the river bank and stood there. I didn't have long to wait. They came creeping through the heavy undergrowth. There were two of them, armed with machine guns. At first I pretended not to see them. On second thoughts, I called out to them: '*Kamerad*!'

They got to their feet and covered me with their guns. One of them called out something to me that didn't sound at all friendly. I wondered what the German was for 'I'm your pal'. I did the next best thing, I smiled like an advert for Colgate's toothpaste and again called out '*Kamerad*!' One of them, his gun pointing straight at me, approached. Then he bent down and began to untangle a spot in the barbed wire fence. Obviously the wire had been cut and camouflaged for such an emergency. He indicated that I come through the hole in the wire. I did so. The other guard came closer and covered me with his gun. Then the first guard crawled through the hole in the wire, threw my bike over the fence, and crawled back again. He carefully replaced the barbed wire strands to camouflage the hole and concealed the bike in the heavy undergrowth. No doubt they would return for the bike. Then he turned his attention to me. He said something that sounded like an order. I just stood there with a stupid smile on my face. He pointed his gun at me and made a gesture I've

72

seen in John Wayne pictures. My hands shot up above my head. He put his gun on the ground and approached. He said something, then kicked my feet apart. While his pal kept me covered, he searched me, removing everything from my pockets. They were both young chaps and while I was being searched I tried to weigh them up. The one doing the frisking seemed the cool deliberate type, but the one covering me with the machine gun was all tensed up. The look on his face told me it wouldn't take much to make him press the trigger. The search completed, the cool one indicated that I start walking. I did so. But my pace was a bit too brisk for them. '*Halt*,' came the order. That word I knew!

I turned. The cool one began a sort of pantomime to indicate that I must slow down my pace. Slowly he lifted one foot high and put it down, then the other foot and put it down. That was easy enough to understand, but I pretended not to. I nodded my head vigorously, turned, and began to walk in the manner indicated. First one foot high, and slowly down; then the other foot high, and slowly down.

'*Nein, nein, nein*,' he roared. And then burst out laughing.

They took me to the nearest watchtower. Soon an army truck arrived and, under heavy escort, I was conveyed to a military establishment some four or five miles behind the border. At the barracks, they took me to an upstairs room. A couple of officers came into the room and conversed with my escort.

'*Americana?*' said one of the officers, smiling pleasantly.

I shook my head.

'*Englander?*'

I shook my head; vigorously.

'Scotland,' I said.

His face lit up. '*Schottlander. Ach so. Schottland!*' He then walked across the floor wailing like a cat and going through the motions of playing an imaginary set of bagpipes. Suddenly he stopped, and pointed to me. '*Schottlander*,' he said triumphantly.

I nodded my head. I felt like the mystery object in the BBC radio game, 'Animal, Vegetable or Mineral'. But they were all quite friendly. My property was returned to me and a meal brought in. It was now quite dark outside. They were waiting for an interpreter to arrive.

I had been quite some time in the room when a high ranking uniformed officer entered. He was middle-aged and spoke English; but not well.

'Why have you come to the German Democratic Republic?' he said.

'I can discuss that only with a senior member of your Security Service,' I replied.

His eyes glinted. 'Come with me,' he said. He took me to a room where a couple of young girls were hammering at typewriters. He said something to them. They got up and left the room. He pointed to a chair vacated by one of the girls.

'Please,' he said. I sat down, but he remained on his feet. 'Are you a soldier?' he asked.

'No,' I replied.

He then told me that he was an officer attached to the State Security and I could disclose to him my reasons for wishing to speak to their Security Service.

'I've come to discuss the rescue of one of your comrades from prison in England,' I said.

He remained silent for a few moments.

'Who is this man?' he asked.

'That's something I don't really know,' I replied. 'In England there are a number of Communists in prison and I wish to know which one I should spring.'

'Can you tell me anything about these Communists? Why are they in prison?'

'They have been convicted of espionage,' I said, avoiding the word spying. I then described how I had escaped from prison in England and had come to discuss the matter of rescuing one of his friends. I kept the story as brief as possible.

'You must go to Berlin. You will leave in the morning.' He picked up the phone and after a brief conversation put down the receiver. 'Do not discuss this matter with anyone until the interpreter arrives.'

I was back in the first room when the interpreter arrived. He was a tall gangling character dressed in civvies and in appearance closely resembled a screw I knew at Scotland's Peterhead prison. This put me off him right away. He explained how his home was some distance from where we were and since he would accompany me to Berlin, he would need to return home in order to pack some clothing for the trip. As he was explaining this to me the middle-aged officer came into the room, held a brief conversation in German and left.

'Now there has been a change of plans,' said the interpreter when the officer had gone. 'We think you should go to another place, tonight. We think you should be taken away from here.'

Ten minutes later I was in the car on the way to some place or other. The interpreter and I sat in the back seat while the middle-aged officer sat in the front beside a uniformed driver. It was a black night and there was little traffic on the road. I have no clear recollections as to how long the journey lasted. Eventually we entered a town and stopped outside what looked like a small tavern.

We entered and found ourselves in a poorly lit hallway. From behind a door in the hallway came the sound of loud conversation and the tinkle of glasses. Some kind of party was going on and as the middle-aged officer opened the door to enter, I caught sight of a number of people, men and women in what was clearly the tavern lounge. In a few moments the middle-aged officer returned with a man of about his own age. There was a whispered conversation and then we all went upstairs. 'This will be your room for tonight,' the interpreter told me. 'You should get some sleep. We leave for Berlin in a few hours. Someone will be outside your door tonight. We must take precautions.'

'What about a nightcap?' I said. I had to explain what a nightcap was.

'I will speak with my chief,' he said, and left the room. In a few seconds he returned to tell me I was being moved to another room; one with a bathroom attached.

'This will make it unnecessary for you to leave the room,' he explained. 'And I will bring you up something to drink.'

When the transfer to the other room had been completed – this was delayed while whoever occupied the other room was moved out – the interpreter appeared with a half bottle of cognac. 'With the compliments of my chief,' he said.

'Look,' I said. 'I don't feel the least bit tired, if you care to have a drink I'd be glad of your company.'

'We thought maybe you were tired,' he said. 'If you are not

going to sleep, my chief would like to ask a few questions. He has a report to make out for the people in Berlin.'

'That's OK by me,' I said.

He opened the door and spoke to someone who was standing outside, then he came back and sat down at the table. I poured a couple of drinks.

'Cheers,' I said.

'You are a member of the – how do you call it? – the Underworld – in England?' asked the interpreter.

'Your chief told me not to discuss myself with anyone,' I said.

'That's all right. I'm a member of the Security Service. And I will be translating for my chief when he comes to see you. You can tell me anything.'

'Yes,' I said. 'I'm a member of the Underworld.'

He leaned across the table and lowering his voice said, 'Do you know Christine Keeler?'

'No,' I told him. 'I don't know her.'

Disappointment clouded his expression. 'What about Mandy? You know, Christine's friend?'

'You mean Mandy Rice Davies? No I don't know her either.' I regretted the answer. I could see he had a real interest in Christine Keeler and Mandy; I don't think his interest was connected with the security of the German Democratic Republic!

Then he wanted to know if I knew any of the Great Train Robbers.

'I'll probably know one or two of them; when they catch them,' I said, in a tone that indicated my reluctance to discuss the matter.

'Do you know anyone who knows Christine Keeler?' he asked hopefully.

I wasn't going to disappoint him this time. 'Sure,' I lied. 'I know a few people who know her very well.'

'Very well!' he said eagerly.

'Sure,' I said. 'Very well!'

His face brightened. 'She is beautiful. Is she not?'

'Not bad,' I said, my manner offhand. I was glad when the middle-aged officer put in an appearance. He arrived when I was in the middle of a story told to me by someone who had been very close to Miss Keeler. The interpreter immediately changed the subject. The middle-aged officer had been drinking and his mood was jovial. It took about an hour to get through the list of questions he had to ask me. When they left the room, I got into bed. I was soon fast asleep.

Next morning we continued to Berlin making one stop on the way. This was at a military prison, quite a large place, the buildings a mixture of very old and modern. I was not taken into the prison block but located in a reasonably furnished room where the interpreter and I ate together.

'You were telling me about your friend and Christine Keeler,' he said once we were alone.

'Oh yes,' I said. 'Now where did I leave off?' I then continued with the pack of lies I had begun the night before. Half an hour later we were again under way. I fell asleep in the car. When I awoke we were in the suburbs of East Berlin. It was to the Prison for State Security that they took me. The sight of the guards armed with machine guns was not encouraging, but the buildings in the background were very modern and looked more like a hospital than a prison.

'We must say goodbye to you here,' said the middle-aged officer. All three shook hands with me. Then a couple of guards ushered me through the side door of a large building. I found myself in a long corridor. The first thing that struck me was the silence. One of the guards beckoned me to follow him along the corridor. Then I saw the cell doors. It was a prison all right; but with a difference. The corridor floor was covered, wall to wall, by a thick carpet. Then, the lights – which had been green in colour – suddenly changed to a dull red. The guard opened a cell door and motioned me inside. He followed me into the cell and indicated that I empty my pockets. He was very polite, even apologetic, in manner. He returned my cigarettes and some cigars, the rest of my property he placed in a large envelope. Then he beckoned me to follow him. This time he led me to a cell directly opposite a flight of wide stone stairs. He motioned me to enter and locked me in. At that moment my feelings were a mixture of resentment and curiosity. Resentment at being locked up; curiosity about the place I was locked up in. The cell was unlike anything I had experienced before. It was spotlessly clean with a highly polished floor. In the wall facing the door were two large

77

windows and in the corner of the cell wall, where the door was, was a lavatory pan. There were two hospital-type beds and a large wardrobe. I didn't know what was next in the programme, but I decided to have a sleep. I stripped off and got into the bed nearest the wardrobe. The sound of a key in the cell door awoke me. A number of soldiers stood around the bed. One of them indicated that I get up and dress. I noticed a tray with food, stood on the table. I felt the teapot. It was stone cold. Someone must have left food when I was asleep. I looked at the window. It was dark outside. I must have been asleep for hours.

'Come,' said one of the guards when I was dressed.

Again the lights were at red. At the end of the corridor hung a large curtain which cut off my view of what lay behind. The guard drew the curtain slightly and peered through. Then he raised his hand to a switch on the wall; the lights in the corridor behind us turned from red to green. The guard motioned me through the curtain, where the lights were still at red. I realized the significance of this. The red lights indicated that a prisoner was out of his cell, the green lights that the corridor was clear. At the other side of the curtain was a stairway. The guard led me up to the second floor, along another corridor till eventually we stopped outside a door bearing the number 344. The guard opened this door to reveal another door: a soundproof room, I thought. The guard pushed open the inner door and motioned me to enter. There were two people in the room. Behind the desk sat a dark-haired, stocky-built man of medium height. At a small table in front of the desk sat a young woman. She was blonde, somewhat plump and quite attractive. The woman – she was there as interpreter – invited me to take a seat opposite her at the table. I was to spend many, many hours at that table during the months ahead. The man behind the table was my interrogator.

The woman introduced the man as Rolf. 'And I am Grace,' she said. She then went on to explain how my unusual entry into the German Democratic Republic made it necessary for them to confirm my identity.

'Why have you come to the GDR?' was the first question put to me. I explained that I wished to know if they were interested in rescuing one of their comrades from prison in England. When she had translated my explanation to Rolf, he made a few hurried notes. 'You travelled all the way to the GDR to ask a question!'

'That's right,' I told her. I did not mention my meetings with Hector back in 1961. After all, although I had been manipulated by Hector to travel to the GDR he had never directly propositioned me, and years of cross-questioning had taught me not to volunteer too much too quickly.

Grace said: 'Sometimes people come to our country for reasons which are not what they claim. Then we find they are not friendly to our country.'

'I'm not a spy, if that's what you mean.'

'We do not know that you are not a spy. And because we do not know anything about you we must take precautions. You understand this, do you not?'

'How long are these questions going to take?' I asked. 'I've left a couple of friends waiting for me in Glasgow; and I've left my luggage in a hotel at Badhersfeld. I didn't plan remaining here for more than a couple of days.'

'The captain, Rolf, says we do not do things the way you seem to think. We must make enquiries and this will take time. We want to know more about you. Is that not reasonable?'

I conceded the point. 'But why do you keep your guests in prison?' I said. 'I've escaped from prison in England to come here and talk to you about rescuing one of your friends. I'm not too happy to find myself in your prison.'

She translated this.

'He says you will be out of this place in a few days. You will go to another place that is not like this. Now let us have the answers to our questions, please,' she said.

The questioning lasted a long time during which there were several breaks for coffee and meals. Rolf knew his job. The questions were well calculated. Had I ever been in contact with anyone who was a member of the British, American or West German Intelligence Service? I truthfully answered, 'No'. They did not dwell on this theme. I got the impression that this type of question was a matter of form. I told them of my association with the British Communist, Peter. Rolf seemed to find this most interesting. The first session in the interrogation room – and it was to be the first of many – lasted many hours and when I returned to the cell I found a meal laid out on the table. After eating I went to bed and was soon fast asleep.

I awoke feeling fresh, got out of bed, dressed myself and was seated at the table when the door opened and a girl soldier entered the cell carrying a meal. She placed the tray on the table and said something in German. I shrugged my shoulders. She went out and closed the door. On the food tray there was something chalked in German, the word *Sonder*. I was to learn later it meant 'special'. As I ate I heard a slight movement outside the cell door. Someone was watching me through the one-way glass of the spyhole. When I finished the meal, the door opened and again the girl soldier entered. She went to the wardrobe, took out a terry towel and a bar of soap. These she handed to me. '*Komm*,' she said. I followed her. She led me along the corridor, opened what looked like a cell door and motioned me to enter. Then she slammed the door shut and locked it. I was in a shower room. I stripped off and began to shower. I wondered if the girl soldier would return and scrub my back. She didn't. From the shower room I was escorted straight back to room 344.

'We want you to write down anything which comes into your head when you are in your room,' – it was never referred to as a cell – said Grace. 'This will shorten the length of time you have to remain in this place.'

'What do you want me to write?' I asked her.

'Write down what you might have to say to us. But you must print everything. Do not put it in your own handwriting, we wish to be sure you are who you claim to be,' she continued, 'and it would help us a great deal if you would write down all the crimes for which you have been convicted; and the crimes for which you have not been convicted.'

This last bit took me by surprise. 'Are you kidding?' I said.

'We don't wish the details,' she hastened to add. 'We just wish to know when and where the crimes were committed. We have ways of checking this.'

I could see the logic of what she said. Someone masquerading as me would take the trouble to memorize the crimes for which I had been convicted. But only the real Patrick Meehan alias Carson, would know the crimes he had committed, but for which he had not been convicted. And – as I saw it – the Press reports on these unsolved crimes would confirm the appropriate dates I gave.

When I got back to the cell after the second interrogation I went through the same procedure as before: eat, sleep, eat, shower and back upstairs to room 344. There was one aspect of their hospitality which I found irksome; I was not allowed to shave. When I complained about it Grace told me, 'There is a reason for this.' After about a week of interrogations, she said: 'When you return to your room you will find a complete set of clothing. You are to change into these and put your own clothing into the case you will find there. Today you are going to another place.'

I pressed her to tell me where I was going. 'I do not know,' was all she would say.

Back in the cell I put on the clothing I found there and packed my own gear into a small soft-topped case. The suit provided was not to my taste; the overcoat would have made a good doormat. None of the clothing was new, except for the shirt and shoes. Then I sat down and waited. They took me, by car, to a nearby airport. Four men travelled with me. Two of these I knew from the interrogation room; Rolf and another youngish man who spoke English, Russian and German. Whether this man was Russian or German is something I never found out. I suspect he was German. The other two in the car, the driver and his seat companion, were middle-aged. When we turned off into the airport, I asked the interpreter where we were going. 'I don't know,' he said. At the airport we entered a long modern-type building and went upstairs and sat down to wait; and a long wait it proved to be. From the window I had a good view of the airport and I watched the planes come and go. While we were sitting there a civilian came in and called Rolf away. He was away for something like half an hour or more and when he returned I could see there was something not to Rolf's liking.

'We must go back,' the interpreter told me.

Downstairs we put the cases into a small van which looked like a caravanette. We returned to the *Hohenschoenhausen* – as my political jail was called – where I changed back into my own clothing. And then they took me into court! The court was a large cell at the far end of the corridor where my cell was situated·

It was the strangest court I've ever attended. The judge was a woman and she sat behind a raised bench smoking. The role of prosecutor was played by a large jovial looking man in military uniform. I was later to meet him and talk with him in room 344. The other persons present in the court were Rolf, Grace and an elderly gentleman who, I suspect, was Rolf's boss. The man in the role of prosecutor spoke good English and he explained what it was all about.

'You are being charged with entering the GDR illegally,' he said. 'But don't let that worry you,' he added, 'you must tell the judge why you entered the GDR.'

I looked across at Grace. 'What will I tell them?' I asked her.

The prosecutor interrupted. 'You must tell them the truth,' he said.

'You mean that I came to the GDR to talk about springing one of your pals from prison? I can't tell the judge a thing like that.'

Grace and the prosecutor went into a fit of laughter. Then, when my remark was translated they all went into a fit of laughter. 'If you have come here to help one of our comrades imprisoned in England, and if you are sincere, the judge will be most understanding.' I then made a brief statement on my reasons for coming to the GDR. When I had finished, the judge looked quite pleased. She held a brief conversation with the prosecutor, I could see she was explaining something to him.

'The judge says,' the prosecutor announced, 'that she is very pleased to know you have come to our country with such good intentions, and she trusts you will understand that we must protect ourselves against persons who come here with not-so-good intentions. Until we have satisfied ourselves of your intentions, you must remain in this place.'

'Bail! What about bail!' I asked the prosecutor. Again Grace and the prosecutor laughed. I was not feeling quite so hilarious, personally. From the courtroom, I was taken upstairs to room 344. The prosecutor was there along with Rolf, Grace and a few others.

'All that was what you call a formality,' the prosecutor told me. 'You would not be here so long; but your business is special, is it not? Maybe you will go to Moscow.'

'I thought I was going somewhere, today,' I said. 'Why did

they take me to the airport, and then bring me back?'

'I don't know,' said the prosecutor. 'That decision was made at the top. Maybe it's a good sign. I think it is.'

'We have a few questions to put to you,' Grace told me, when the prosecutor left the room. From behind his desk, Rolf began to speak. Grace to translate. The questions were all to do with Peter. Could I recall any conversations I had had with Peter? What did I say in these conversations, and what did Peter say? Who were Peter's friends? When did I write to Peter from prison, and what did I say in the letter? This line of questioning, at last, was encouraging. Obviously, they were trying to establish if I really did know Peter. Just as obviously, they would have methods of contacting Peter who, I was sure, would speak well of me. Perhaps I was getting through the red-tape barrier.

I pondered on what I should tell them about Hector. Should I mention him at all? After all, I knew absolutely nothing about him. I had no name, no address, no evidence to prove that he was what I suspected him to be: a Communist intelligence agent. To repeat our conversations verbatim – or as near to verbatim as I could remember – would only be to repeat a few lines of superficially casual chatter. As the words would look on paper, Hector had asked me to do nothing. He may have planted some ideas, but they had flowered in my own mind. And I had just experienced a 'show trial' – a formality, they had said. But if that woman judge had decided she did not like my answers, what powers did she have to impose a 'formal' sentence – like twenty years in the salt mines? That might be a formality to an Iron Curtain judge, but it would be very, very real for the poor so-and-so who had to serve out the years. I was beginning to realize that I had set off on a course across some very troubled waters. Question was: was I already out of my depth?

In Britain, lawyers have a dictum that you never ask a witness a question to which you don't already know the answer; something unexpected can ruin your case. Seen from the other viewpoint – the criminal viewpoint – this dictum still holds true: never tell an interrogator anything he doesn't already know, otherwise you might unwittingly ruin your own defence. If Hector was one of their men, I decided, let them raise the matter themselves. It was the only card I had to keep up my sleeve.

8 A prison is a prison is a . . .

As the days passed into weeks and the weeks into months, I began
to curse my own boundless optimism. I must have been mad, I
realized, to have thought that I could float into East Berlin, spend
a few days in urgent consultation – the subject of which would be
how to spring a Communist spy from one of HM's prisons – and
then float out again. I had forgotten the curse of the 'civilized'
world: bureaucracy; and was soon to learn that the red-tape
weavers of Britain work at hand-loom pace compared with the
Communists. They have whole factories churning out the stuff.
Even if they don't strangle their poor subjects in it – and that is
more by luck than judgement – they leave them bound, gagged
and blindfolded. In the meantime, a prison is a prison is a prison,
even though there are carpets on the floor and the guards ask you
politely if you would accompany them back to your 'room' rather
than your 'cell'.

The questioning in room 344 went on endlessly, but the mere
answering of questions was much too simple for the teutonic
minds of my 'hosts'. I had to write down anything I could think
of, endless essays about prisons in Britain, about methods of
'tapping' corrupt guards, ways and means of smuggling equipment in to prisoners. One of their obsessions seemed to be establishing a regular contact with their people inside: not the normal
methods of whispered messages at visiting times, or laboriously
smuggled letters, these were far too indirect. Why not put a telephone in their cells? I suggested one day. They didn't laugh. I
did, however, put forward a suggestion which seemed to interest
them: why not smuggle in a two-way radio? A very good idea,
they said, but how could it be done? That answer was simplicity
itself: send in two identical transistor radios, one to the spy, one
to a humble ordinary prisoner. Transistors are a permitted
'luxury' in most prisons; but a set presented to a convicted spy
would obviously be subjected to the closest scrutiny. So he or
she – I did not know at this time that Helen Kroger was not one

of the targets – would receive a perfectly standard piece of equipment. It was the set sent to the ordinary-class prisoner that would be 'doctored' to transmit as well as receive, a piece of technology well within the reach of the most humble security service. After a few days, the two radios would be switched, with or without the knowledge of the straight convict. Someone would have to enter his cell while he was on a working party and simply change the serial numbers on the two radios – these are usually mounted on a screw-on plate. Entering the cell would be no problem, either: there are men in every nick in Britain who can float in and out of cells with more ease than a ghost walking through a wall. I wrote a lot of essays about transistor radios! I also drew plans of every prison I knew, and went into great length about their physical weak spots. Most window bars, for instance, are made from soft steel, no obstacle at all to a man with a few hacksaw blades. Better still, the window casings tend to be made of cast-iron, which can be broken with one sharp blow from a heavy object wrapped in cloth to deaden the crack.

Crooked or bent warders also interested them a great deal, but it was a subject they took to with little conviction. I don't suppose there are many behind the iron curtain – a firing-squad would be their deterrent. They wanted to know how contact would be made with a bent screw, and didn't believe how easy it could be. The simplest way, of course, is through fellow inmates. Every nick I have been in has what is virtually an unwritten filing cabinet on the staff: so-and-so is a vicious brute, keep out of his way; so-and-so else is a pansy, so watch him; so-and-so the other is bent, but his prices are high. Often, the contact is made by the screw himself – some are so greedy that they can't wait for the normal prison grapevine to trickle the message out. I told them of one meeting with crooked warders which took place in Nottingham prison. One warder approached me as soon as he heard that I had a fair reputation as a peterman – one of the types of criminals who is not short of friends outside with ready cash. If I wanted anything, he whispered, winking theatrically, I just had to arrange for a letter to be sent to a nearby pub he used. Sure, I replied, I needed some cigarettes, a half bottle of whisky and some ready cash for every day prison transactions. MacTampson immediately despatched £25 to the Nottingham pub. A day or so later, my bent screw came into the cell and slipped me £12 in notes.

'There you are, Jock,' he said – any Scot in an English jail is called Jock – 'delivery as promised. The whisky is in the dustbin.'

He left, locked the cell behind him and I began to hide the money. I heard the key in the lock again and turned. My face must have dropped because standing in the doorway was another screw.

'What's up with you then, Jock?' he smirked. 'You look as though I've caught you in the act stealing the Crown Jewels.' My £12 in change was still lying on the top of the bed. He picked it up and waved it in my face, glowering blackly. 'So you've been at it already, have you Jock?' he went on. 'This is a bad business – it's going to lose you six months remission at least.' I knew he was speaking the truth. Possessing large sums of money – and £12 was large by prison standards then – was a serious offence for it was *ipso facto* evidence that a man had been corrupting screws: there was no other way of getting the money in. (Very little happened to the screws, incidentally.)

'It's a bit of a shame, really,' my man was going on. 'I know you're a villain, Meehan, but you're a clean one by all accounts. It seems a shame to hammer you on a thing like this . . .' I said nothing. I thought it was a shame, too – a bloody shame – but I wasn't going to beg for mercy. He cleared his throat and went on: 'As far as I know, it's the first time you have put a foot wrong here. I'll tell you what I'll do . . . we'll forget the whole business if you let me donate this to charity.' Again he waved the notes. I grinned inwardly: I knew what charity he meant – his own drinking money fund! But I only grinned inwardly. Six months is a lot of remission to lose. I said solemnly: 'If you would do that, sir, I would be very obliged.'

'Right,' he said, pocketing the money with alacrity, 'this time we'll forget all about it.' A few days later, I got the word from my fellow prisoners: the 'double take' was a standard rip-off organized by those two screws working together. One took the money in – at a price. The second confiscated it. Still, they didn't take the whisky. I retrieved it from the dustbin that night.

I gave the East Germans a long list of bent English screws –

very long, considering the small amount of time I had spent behind bars south of the border. I wonder what the British Home Office would have done with that list? I knew what the East Germans would do – and may have done a year or so later. First they would try a small amount of money to 'persuade' a bent screw to help an ordinary category prisoner. The transaction would be tape-recorded, perhaps even photographed by a secret camera. Then the blackmail would start: help one of our spies, or the evidence goes to the Home Office. I had no scruples at all in handing this information to the Communists. To be totally honest, I relished the idea. Too many prisoners I knew have been driven to the very edge of madness or worse by the blackmailing demands of unscrupulous warders. It was time the worm turned.

So my interrogations went on: endless questions, endless essays. I repeated the same information time and time again; time and time again I was asked to repeat it 'just once more'. It is difficult to know whether they believed it or not. They would have disbelieved George Washington, even if he had been born a Russian and chopped down his cherry tree in the grounds of the Kremlin. They soon began to 'plant' other prisoners in my cell, as though I had never heard of the word 'informer'.

He said his name was Gerhard Hohner, and he came from Bitterfeld, GDR. He said he had been arrested for industrial espionage. He said quite a lot about himself; but it is unlikely that any of it was true. He was what the Germans call *ein Spitzel*, a police spy. He spoke English with a marked American accent; but his grasp of the language was perfect. He told me his lies, I told him mine. My lies were much more modest than his: I had been taken off the Frankfurt West Berlin train because I had lost my passport. My name was Martin Dunlievy, a Scotsman, but my home was in Canada. I was suspicious of him from the word go. After three, maybe four days I was quite certain that he was a plant.

'So what!' I told myself. 'I've got nothing to hide.'

It was around the second day of his coming to the cell that things began to happen. About an hour after lunch, it was. We were sitting on our beds talking across to each other. Suddenly, I doubled up with a pain in the pit of my stomach.

'Is there something wrong?' he asked.

I couldn't answer. I got to my feet and moved like a streak of lightning. My timing was perfect. As I reached the lavatory pan, my trousers round my ankles, my guts fell out. I could actually feel myself shrinking and was sure that in a few minutes I would disappear. The thought occurred to me that when I was gone Gerhard would simply get up and pull the chain. Then, as suddenly as it had started, the attack was over.

'What is wrong with you?' said Gerhard. I noticed that he never took his eyes off me.

'There must have been something wrong with the meat we had for lunch,' I told him, as I sat down on the bed again. 'What about you. How do you feel?' I asked.

'I think you're right,' he said, screwing his face up. 'I can feel a pain coming on.' At that moment the cell door opened and a guard appeared. '*Komm*,' he said, pointing to me.

When I got back to the cell, Gerhard was stretched out on his bed reading.

'How's the stomach?' I asked.

'Right now I'm fine, but I was really bad after you were taken away.'

The following night, after supper, we were again seated on our beds chatting when I felt myself getting drowsy.

'I'm going to turn in. I'm tired,' I told him.

'I'm tired, too,' said Gerhard.

I got into bed and dropped off as soon as my head hit the pillow. During the night I came to a half-awake state. I could hear myself talking. I opened my eyes. Gerhard was standing at my bedside, talking to me. Next morning I awoke to the sound of myself singing. Later that day I broached the subject with Gerhard.

'Last night I woke up and found you at my bed talking to me.'

'You must have dreamt it,' he said, laughing.

'Maybe you're right,' I said.

But I knew it had been no dream. I recalled how the drowsiness of the previous night had come upon me too suddenly. I had been drugged and interrogated in my sleep! It occurred to me that, since I had been singing in my sleep, this might indicate to

Rolf and his friends that I had a clear conscience, even if I were a rotten singer! Then I thought about my panic leap onto the lavatory pan. My food had been doctored too.

'Did you hear about the Americans tapping the phone wires?' said Gerhard, one day.

'What was that about?' I asked.

'Didn't you hear about it? They dug a tunnel from West Berlin.'

'Yes,' I said, 'I remember reading about it.'

'It was an East Berlin road worker who found it,' said Gerhard. 'He was digging up the roadway when all of a sudden he fell into the tunnel. Very clever those Americans.'

'That wasn't the story I read in the British Press,' I said. 'Didn't some double agent tip-off the Russians? Guy named Blake.'

'I have not heard about this,' said Gerhard. 'This Blake. Who is he?'

'A British Intelligence Agent,' I said. 'He was working for the Russians. Got forty-two years in prison for it. The judge must think Blake is a *turtle* to live that long.'

'Forty-two years,' said Gerhard. 'You must be joking. Do they really give out such long sentences in England?' He continued to keep on the subject of Blake. I came to the conclusion that he was sounding out my views on Blake's betrayal of British and American agents. I took care to express views that were sympathetic to Blake. Grace was no longer my interpreter. A young chap who spoke English, German and Russian took her place. Only when he was not available did Grace put in an appearance.

In the cell, Gerhard was undergoing a change of personality – perhaps I should say 'a change of sex'. In the shower room were two sprays, both in working order. But Gerhard would keep coming under my spray, and stick his backside against me. In the interrogation room I asked the interpreter: 'What's the German word for poof?'

'*Warmer Bruder*' (warm brother) said the interpreter. 'Why do you ask?'

'The man in my cell,' I said. 'He's red hot.'

'How do you get along with him?' asked the interpreter.

'Not as well as he would like,' I said. 'But he's not a bad chap.'

'What do you talk about when you are together?'

'Oh,' I said. 'We get along fine. I tell him my lies and he tells me his.'

'How do you know that he tells you lies?' asked the interrogator.

'Because he is a spy for you,' I replied. When this was translated, Rolf made a pretence at anger. 'Look,' I said. 'I don't know what's going on. I'm not a spy. But if you put Grace in my room for the night, I'll confess to anything you want.'

On my return to the cell the evening meal was already on the table. 'You look like a spy,' I said to Gerhard, jokingly.

'How do you know what a spy looks like?' said Gerhard, not missing a trick. We were still eating when the cell door opened and Gerhard was called out. I never saw him again.

By this time, the dullness of East German prison routine, even in the *Hohenschoenhausen*, had become as crushing as the dullness of British prison routine. The first stimulating feeling of a new escapade had gone: counter intelligence agents were about as exciting as bank clerks, I decided. There were a few flashes of excitement, however. One day in the interrogation room, I spotted a photograph on Rolf's desk, a photograph which looked strangely familiar. I maintained Rolf's interest by talking to him in German – I had been studying the language as soon as I arrived behind the Curtain, and was getting quite good – as I studied the picture from the corner of my eye. Then it clicked it was Donald Whittaker, one of the men who had escaped with me from Nottingham prison.

'Donald Whittaker,' I said, smiling. 'That's Donald Whittaker.'

There was a hurried discussion between Rolf and the interpreter, in German so fast I could not follow. The interpreter turned and said solemnly: 'You are mistaken.' The photograph was pushed into a folder and never mentioned again. Was I meant to see it or not? I will never know, but it gave me some encouragement that things were still moving – moving with the speed of a crippled snail, but moving nevertheless.

It was the first week of December. The cell door opened and the guard entered carrying a case. The case contained the clothing I wore on my day out at the airport. The guard left me to get on

90

with it. I changed and packed my own clothing into the case. It was early afternoon. The cell door opened again: '*Komm.*' Rolf and a lieutenant went with me in the car.

'*Wohin*?' (where to) I asked.

'Scotland Yard,' said Rolf, a mischievous glint in his eye. It was one of the few English expressions he knew.

At the airport we went upstairs to the same room as before. But not for long. A few minutes later we were walking across the tarmac to the plane. There were children in the plane, calling out to one another in Russian. I tried to take a window seat, but Rolf beat me to it. I settled down, flanked by Rolf and the lieutenant. The lieutenant took some reading material from a briefcase and handed me a magazine. The magazine was illustrated with English, German and Russian print below each plate. It was full of photographs of the German concentration camps. We took off and I looked out of the window. The position of the sun told me we were flying east. Rolf produced a hip flask and three plastic containers. '*Prost!*' The lieutenant clicked his container against mine and we threw back our drinks.

'Scotland Yard,' said Rolf, poker-faced.

'*Springe aus dem Fenster,*' I told him in German (jump out of the window). Rolf smiled.

I fell asleep and woke up with my ears crackling. We landed and the lieutenant told me that we must wait until the rest of the passengers had disembarked. It was dark outside and cold. We descended the gangway and got into a waiting van. A civilian – one of the reception committee of three – got into the van with us. The lieutenant and the civilian talked in Russian. The civilian shook hands with Rolf and me. The van became mobile, then came to a stop. The door opened and Rolf and the lieutenant got out leaving me with the civilian. Through the open van door I could see that we were in a large shed, or hangar. I saw a fire hydrant and above it a sign in the Russian language. I recalled the prosecutor's words: 'You will go to Moscow.' The van door was slammed shut. The civilian smiled and said something in Russian. I couldn't understand a word. I shrugged my shoulders and smiled back. A few minutes later the van door opened and Rolf and the lieutenant, assisted by another member of the reception committee, loaded in the luggage.

It took a couple of hours to get to wherever it was they took me. When we got there I could tell – I've had the experience several times – that we were entering some kind of gate. Once out of the van, a few short steps took us into a large modern building. It was to another cell that they took me – furnished, but still a cell. The window had the same small opaque panes as the ones in the *Hohenschoenhausen*. In addition, the casement was sealed off by mesh wires flush with the inside wall. But there was an added luxury, a reading lamp on a small sidetable. The cell was located in a short corridor on the third or fourth floor of the building. In the corridor were twelve doors, six on each side; but they were not all cell doors, as I found out later. Within minutes of my arrival in the cell, a woman brought in a meal; fish (still in the tin), black bread and lemon tea. The woman – heavily built, wearing a white cotton coat – put the tray on the table and left without a word. I ate the bread but not the fish, it was too salty.

About an hour elapsed, then they came for me. We went down a flight of stairs to another corridor, and I found myself in a large, richly-furnished room. Six or eight persons, at least two of them women, were in the room. Behind a desk sat a heavily-built, middle-aged man dressed – as all the others were – in mufti. At each side of the desk, and close against it, were typists' tables. Rolf and the lieutenant were present; but the interpreting was done, not by the lieutenant, but by an elderly woman who wore her hair in a bun at the back of her head. The stage was set for an interrogation. The man behind the desk (I believe his rank was that of colonel; but I was never told this officially) said a few words, then the interpreter addressed me politely.

'Was there something wrong with the fish?'

I explained that I didn't like fish and left it at that.

The next question was the one I had answered so often before: 'Why did you come to the German Democratic Republic?'

I gave the same answer: 'To talk about rescuing one of your comrades from prison in England.'

The colonel beamed at me from behind his desk. 'Glasgow Rangers,' he said. I smiled and nodded knowingly. The colonel said something to the interpreter.

'He says Glasgow Rangers is a good football team,' said the interpreter.

I explained that I had no interest in football, but agreed that Glasgow Rangers was a good team, nearly as good as Celtic. With a name like Patrick Connolly Meehan I felt obliged to plug for Celtic even if I were an atheist. That first interview, like the ones that followed over the next couple of weeks, was quite brief. Nearly all the questions put to me were a rehash of those asked in East Berlin. I found myself wondering why they should take the trouble to bring me all this way just to ask me the same old questions. It didn't make sense. Although never told where I was – for some reason this was to be kept secret from me – I was never in any doubt that I was in Russia: probably Moscow. On one occasion when I raised the matter with the lieutenant he told me there were many parts of the German Democratic Republic where the Russian comrades were stationed. This, he explained, was necessary to protect the democratic countries of the East against possible capitalist aggression. The lieutenant did not say that I was still in the GDR but that was the inference. For a couple of weeks or so I was seldom allowed to exercise in the open air (a couple of times I was allowed out onto a flat roof that was enclosed by a twelve-foot wall) and I mentioned this to the woman interpreter. The following day I was allowed the use of a billiard room for a couple of hours, a gesture intended to placate me perhaps. But knocking billiard balls around under the eyes of an armed guard – dressed in a Russian military uniform – isn't exactly recreation. After half an hour I sat down near one of the heavily curtained windows. This – for some reason which I never was able to fathom – caused the guard to become agitated. He picked up a phone and spoke a few words. Soon afterwards a young woman appeared, dressed in military uniform. She took down a cue and laughingly indicated that she wished to join me in a game. She was quite attractive and I could think of better games to play with her, and when I realized she didn't know a word of English, I told her so in English.

We spent about an hour knocking the balls around and – knowing she had no English – I used some rather impolite expressions when I failed to pot a ball. One expression I habitually used was 'fucking hell.' After a few 'fucking hells' – I'm not a very good billiard player – the girl joined in the spirit of things and began to mimic me. This doubled me up with laughter and – since she had been sent up to entertain me – I encouraged her to use the expression. Since she was a more hopeless player than me, she used it quite often. There was to be a sequel the following day when in the interrogation room, the colonel decided to have a coffee break. After break the same girl came into the room to collect the dishes. As she was putting the cups on the tray, held balanced on one hand, one of the cups slipped from her grasp.

'Fucking hell,' she gasped.

At this I fell-to with laughter. But the woman interpreter was not amused. With difficulty the lieutenant managed to keep a straight face – but only just. 'Does she know English?' the woman interpreter asked me.

'Yes,' I told her. 'She speaks English quite well.'

'But what she said just now is not very polite. Is it?'

'Not really,' I replied. 'But I don't mind.'

Later, when the woman interpreter was out of the room, the colonel questioned the lieutenant on the matter. 'Have you been teaching the girl English?' the lieutenant asked.

I then explained how the girl had picked up the expression from me. When this was translated for the colonel, he too roared with laughter. The next time I saw the girl was in the cell corridor. I gave her a friendly wave which she returned and in a voice that was not too loud she called out 'fucking hell' and then waved her fist at me in pretended anger. I suspect the woman interpreter had had a word with her about her English. A few days before Christmas I was returned to the *Hohenschoenhausen*. On the plane coming back I learned something that the whole world had known for weeks – President Kennedy had been assassinated in Dallas.

9 Spies, big and small

Decades, I suppose, mean all things to all men. We all have very personal reasons for remembering, say, the Thirties and the Forties, apart from depression and war. But in the public mind, decades become linked with some mood or event, or series of events, like the 'Roaring Twenties' people older than me reminisce about. The 1960s were the years of The Beatles and Swinging London, of a victorious English World Cup team and of the acrid political battles between Harold Wilson and Ted Heath. They were also the years of the Spy.

Burgess and Maclean had started it all in the early Fifties, when these ex-public-school pillars of the establishment suddenly pulled up roots and fled to Moscow. They left an embarrassed secret service claiming that theirs had been the only major infiltration of the nation's secret centres. The public goggled and then forgot about it. As the new decade arrived, however, appetites for espionage and intrigue were whetted once again as the first James Bond books began their climb up the bestseller charts round the world. It was only fiction, of course! It didn't really happen! – despite the fact that Ian Fleming was a wartime security man who rose to be personal assistant to the Director of Naval Intelligence.

Fiction became fact with a bang. First came the Portland spy trial, when the public became painfully aware that the KGB – the Russian intelligence network – not only *existed* in real life, but was *active*: stealing submarine detection secrets from the Portland Underwater Research Centre, secrets of the gravest importance in the era of the submarine-launched intercontinental ballistic missile. The names of spies became as famous as those of popstars: Gordon Lonsdale, real name Konon Molody (or was it Konstantine Ladeinkov?), the top KGB agent who organized the ring; Helen and Peter Kroger, the scholarly bookshop owners who in fact ran the communication network for the ring; Henry Houghton, the former Admiralty clerk, and his hapless fiancée Ethel Gee, the couple who actually handed over the secrets. At the end of their sensational trial, Lonsdale was sentenced to 25 years, the Krogers 22 years, and Houghton and Gee 15 years. If the public thought it was over, they were terribly wrong. It was only the beginning.

A year later, the pathetic figure of William John Christopher Vassall shuffled into the limelight, a homosexual clerk at the British Embassy in Moscow. He got too drunk at a party one night, and lived to regret it. The KGB had photographed him in indecent positions with another man, and the blackmail screws went on. Vassall drew 18 years. In 1963, more holes were revealed in the British security colander: Harold 'Kim' Philby, the Third Man in the Burgess-and-Maclean affair, also fled to Russia. At one time, he had been the head of the anti-Communist section of British Intelligence – and his orders came from the Kremlin! Was this the greatest espionage coup of all time? By this time, an odd figure had stumbled into the fringes of this dark and sinister jungle – me!

A few chance remarks – or they seemed like chance remarks at the beginning – outside Glasgow General Post Office seemed destined to whisk me from the comparative cosiness of the Glasgow underworld into something much deeper, darker and more dramatic. Something potentially profitable too, for a man with Communist leanings and an urgent desire for a large sum of money, quickly, in order to establish a new life for himself and his family. At the time I had those two strange meetings with Hector, the most sensational trial of them all was still in the future – double agent George Blake was yet to be arrested. We were due to end up behind the bars of different English prisons for very different offences: me for trying to blow a safe in a Co-op, he for betraying forty British agents to his KGB colleagues while working for the British Foreign Office. I was to get 5 years, he 42! Blake and I were never to meet, but the threads of our lives were to cross – manipulated by hidden fingers.

These, then, were the spies whose activities in Britain caused much private soul-searching within the security services, and much public outcry in Parliament and the Press – at one stage, there was even serious talk that the recurring scandals would bring down the Government. Meanwhile, in my claustrophobic

Patrick Connelly Meehan

Detective Chief Superintendent David Struthers, who was in charge of the Ayr murder investigation which led to Meehan's wrongful conviction

Meehan's notebook with notations of the torn out page, signed by Senior Prison Officer Davidson of Peterhead Prison

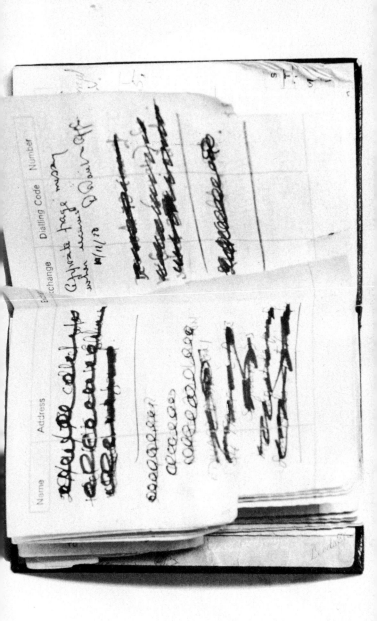

Detective Superintendent Cowie

below The Free Paddy Meehan Committee.
From left to right Joseph Beltrami, Ross Harper, Ludovic Kennedy,
David Burnside, Leonard Murray

above The two *Scottish Daily News* reporters, George Forbes (left) and Jack Wallace, who did a great deal to uncover evidence that cleared Meehan and Griffiths of the murder

The two police officers whose investigations led to the arrest of Ian Waddell: John McDougal (left) and Arthur Bell

Paddy Meehan, his wife Betty and son Gary on the day the Queen's Pardon was granted

little world at the *Hohenschoenhausen*, I was having my own problems with spies – not international operators from the James Bond world, but seedy little men 'planted' in my cell as *Spitzels* – informers. I suppose all policemen are bound to have suspicious minds – they couldn't do their job otherwise. Political policemen are probably more suspicious than their 'criminal' colleagues. But it would appear that a Communist political policeman is the most suspicious man in the world. They certainly seemed to have doubts about my story. Presumably, they believed I was an MI5 'plant'. So there came a series of successors to Gerhard.

I like to think that I spotted them straight away; I adopted a policy of telling them the wildest lies about my name, my background, anything that came into my head. To be honest, inventing some of the stories gave me great pleasure – it came very close to creative writing, after all. What Rolf and my other interrogators thought of the information that came back from their *Spitzels* I will never know because, of course, they always denied they were using spies.

'We would not do a thing like that,' Rolf would say, pan-faced.

Seeing that their planted cell-mates were meeting with little success, they moved into another sphere of activity – wall-tapping. The men who run prisons throughout the world seem to be terrified of the thought of communication between their charges. Many forbid conversation; all – to my knowledge at least – forbid 'tapping', the knocking out of messages on cell walls or ceilings to neighbouring inmates. To my knowledge also, every prisoner in the world ignores this ban. Wall-tapping, without a knowledge of morse code, is a laborious process. The simplest greeting takes a great deal of time – but then, of course, the one thing prisoners have plenty of is time. Nevertheless, there is a shorthand method which obviates the necessity to knock twenty-six times to communicate the letter Z. This is the chessboard method, when the first row of eight squares is given the letters from A to H, the second row I to P and so on. A becomes two knocks, with a slight pause in between: row one, square one. Z is four knocks, pause, and two: row four, square two. It is, as I have said, still a laborious process, and for me it was made doubly difficult because most of my communication had to be in German. I was studying the language, and had plenty of time to practise during my interrogations and telling my lies to my *Spitzels*, but have you ever seen the length of some German words? Nevertheless, I soon built up a quite extensive tapping network, particularly with the cell directly above me – which was in the women's section. There are easier and much more satisfying ways of enjoying your sex-life than tapping a spoon on concrete, but beggars ... etc, etc. It is better to talk to a woman than to have nothing to do with a woman whatsoever.

Over the months, I established close contacts with some of my 'ladyfriends' upstairs. I still, in fact, write to two of them. Their stories were often quite horrifying, for they faced soul-destroying sentences for offences which we would consider to be quite trivial. Most of them were 'inside' for wishing to satisfy that basic human need, to travel. Trouble was, most of them wanted to travel to West Berlin – on false papers! Any lofty ideas I still had about the ennobling effect of Communism on the human condition left me during these long tapped-out 'conversations'. I threw out Communism – at least as practised in East Germany – to join my long-discarded Catholicism.

Perhaps the saddest case of all was that of Beatte Barwich, who became a political prisoner at the age of nineteen simply because she was the daughter of a brilliant scientist. Her father, Heinz Barwich, was the physicist who defected to the West while attending a peace conference in Geneva. She and her brother Peter were immediately arrested and charged with having false papers – although Beatte had never seen these. The SD – the *Staatsicherherheitsdienst*, or state security service – told her that they had discovered the papers in Peter's possession. As she was never allowed to see her brother, she was unable to check this allegation. She wondered what was to become of her. I wondered too. Our communications had to be guarded, because we thought the guards might be listening in to our 'tapping' talks. And Beatte herself was given several suspicious cell-mates who might also be 'plants'.

My doubts about the security of tapping had been increased by several strange messages I had received. One came in a way that completely baffled me – until I realized it was in English. And it enquired: 'Are you called Meehan?'

The query came with all the shock of a cold shower, for in all my 'talks' to neighbouring cells I had used the name of Dunlievy. I tapped back 'No' and let the matter rest.

It was the discovery of the 'toilet telephone' that helped the friendship between myself and Beatte flower. One morning while my cell-mate – another *Spitzel* – was cleaning our lavatory with a large brush, he accidentally, or so it seemed, forced all the water over the S-bend. We were sitting there when the cell was suddenly filled with a loud rushing sound. It took me a few seconds to realize what had happened: one of the girls upstairs had pulled the chain of their toilet, and we could hear the water rushing past our empty pipe. So the systems were connected! Hurriedly, I tapped out the puzzling message: 'Empty the water from your toilet.' Not surprisingly, I had to repeat it several times before we began to hear water surging down the pipe.

Excitedly, I put my head down the pan and whispered: 'Can you hear me?'

'Yes – loud and clear,' the answer boomed back. It was probably loud and clear in West Berlin too, for it would appear that lavatories also make excellent megaphones.

'Shhhh,' I shushed, and our first excited conversation began.

The description may conjure a strange picture in the mind of the reader – a Gorbals villain and an excited East German teenager, laughing and giggling as they both knelt with their heads down lavatory pans. But to me, it was the greatest breakthrough in communications since Marconi invented the radio.

While my social chit-chat had suddenly gained this new dimension, my interrogations in room 344 were beginning to get more and more involved. I was still answering interminable questions about the English prison system, still writing copious essays, but more and more often I was being faced with different – and probably more senior – interrogators. They had a habit of dropping vital pieces of information as casual asides and observing my reactions closely.

It was in this way I learned that Gordon Lonsdale was in the GDR after his exchange for the British spy, Greville Wynne. This gem was mentioned casually a few weeks after I was questioned by a group of people I had not met before. Although one of them asked most of the questions, and appeared to be the leader of the group, he kept shooting telling glances at a small, rather swarthy man who sat quietly on the edge of the group. Earlier that day I had seen this same man in the corridor of the prison as I was marched past. He gave me a long and piercing perusal. As I sat in room 344, I could sense something false about the atmosphere: there was an air of deference towards this swarthy man, although superficially he was not considered important enough to ask me any questions.

The swarthy man was Lonsdale, called as an observer to judge the accuracy and honesty of my replies based on his own prison experiences in England. But it was only when I got back to London I realized the identity of the man. I saw a photograph of him in a book or magazine. Typically, the East Germans made no effort to tell me his name, much less introduce me.

There were other pennies to drop as the endless questioning went on. One morning, Rolf and the lieutenant began to express an intense interest in Sheila, the dark-haired lady who had driven me to the last disastrous Co-op raid.

'Did she volunteer to drive you, or did you ask her to do it?'

'She volunteered.'

Rolf and the lieutenant exchanged knowing glances.

'Do you think there was a tip-off?' asked the lieutenant.

'There could have been, I have no evidence one way or the other.'

'When you escaped from Nottingham jail, how did you know that Sheila was in Spain?'

'I didn't know – I was just told that by a young fellow who went to fetch her.'

'Did Sheila know that your passport was being collected in Nottingham and taken to London for you?'

'She might have done if she'd been there,' I answered, with less conviction. 'But she was in Spain.'

'You don't really know she was in Spain, do you?'

'No – I suppose not.'

'Yet the lady who brought your passport from Nottingham was followed by a police car which was later discovered to have come from Scotland Yard?'

'Yes, I've already told you that.'

I looked at them.

'You think that Sheila is an informer, don't you?' I asked.

Rolf, as usual, would not give a straight reply. He merely said: 'Perhaps you should become more careful how you choose your friends.'

I didn't need the advice. I had already realized I must have been mad to have dismissed the obvious for so long.

Another gem of information, which caused me a surge of very real anger, was mentioned conversationally during another lengthy interrogation.

'By the way,' said my questioner, a Herr Ullbrich, who pretended to be a Communist equivalent of a British prison visitor, 'the British know you are in the GDR.'

I exploded: 'If they know that, you must have told them . . .'

I was furious. I hoped the police back home would have assumed I had gone back to Canada. What was the point of my going back to England to help plot a jail break to face authorities who knew I had been behind the Curtain? A schoolboy could add that particular two and two: I had returned to spring a spy.

'Why did they tell the bastards?' I demanded to know.

Herr Ullbrich was calm: 'Perhaps it is better this way. You would only have been picked up eventually in any case.'

The logic of that answer stopped me in my tracks: *Pow!* So not only had they told the British Home Office; they also intended to hand me back to the police, instead of putting me back over the border secretly as I had hoped. I was going to swop a Kraut jail for a Sassenach jail as a reward for all my troubles.

'You double-dealing bastards!' I shouted.

Herr Ullbrich took it all very coolly – as well he might, for he could walk out of prison any time he wanted.

'You will understand the necessity,' he went on calmly. 'If we were to let you go secretly, the British authorities would immediately suspect our plans. If we hand you over officially, saying we held you for entering our country without a passport, they will have no cause for concern.'

He was right, of course. The so-and-so's always were. But once again, my plans for the Big One had gone horribly awry!

*

I was to undergo one more delight during my 'visit' behind the Iron Curtain. It came in the shape of a six-foot Egyptian maniac by the name of Hamdy. He hated Germans and had a very abrupt way of expressing that hatred. I was the only other non-German in the prison at that time, so it was deemed necessary that we should become cell-mates. The only good thing I can say about Hamdy is that he was certainly no *Spitzel*. He came into the cell as I was on the 'telephone' to Beatte. As soon as the guard left, I stuck my head back down the pan and gabbled away. Hamdy sat on the bed, looking somewhat more than puzzled.

'Are you sick?' he asked when the conversation was over.

'No,' I said, and went to bed. I laughed hysterically under the sheets: Hamdy looked a very worried man. I left my explanation until the following morning. He looked more than relieved – and demanded to speak to Beatte.

'I'm very big, very broad and very good looking,' he lied into the pan. He added truthfully: 'I hate Germans.'

Beatte, a good Kraut despite her problems, pulled the chain. The Egyptian shot to his feet, his face a mask of glowering menace. He crossed to the table, picked up my bread-knife and began sharpening it on the window sill.

'I hate Germans,' he said.

'Me too,' I said. I was prepared to hate anyone he hated.

'The last cell I was in, I kicked the door right off its hinges,' he said. I laughed – hoping it was the right thing to do.

'Then I threw the other man out into the corridor.' He meant his cell-mate. There's one thing, I told myself, if he kicks the door off this cell he won't have to throw me out. I'll be out like a shot – voluntarily!

He began to feel the cutting edge of the knife with his thumb. 'Sharp,' he said, and threw the knife on the table. He took a running-jump at the door. It sounded like a stick of gelignite going off inside my eardrum. But the door held. He moved back for another run. There was the sound of voices outside the cell door. The spyhole moved. Hamdy flew at the door and I could see daylight round the edges. He moved back for another run, but at that moment the door opened and they came in. There were so many of them I didn't bother to count. They pounced on him, forced him to the floor and held him while a male nurse injected him with some kind of sedative. Within minutes he was asleep. They picked him up and placed him on the bed. Then they left, locking the door.

Beatte gave me the signal to get on the phone.

'What's all the noise about?' she wanted to know.

I told her Hamdy was a bit upset.

'He must be mad,' said Beatte.

I didn't want to upset her so I didn't say that Hamdy was unconscious on the bed. 'He's gone upstairs for an interview,' I lied.

'Did you hear him describe himself to me?' Beatte said.

'Yes, I heard him,' I said. 'But he lied. He is not tall and handsome. He is small, bow-legged, has a hump and a bald head.'

Beatte laughed. 'Is that the truth?' she asked.

I heard the key hit the cell lock. I got up and pulled the chain. A guard entered. '*Komm,*' he said.

When I reached room 344, Rolf was alone. I asked him what his game was. Why had he put a madman in the cell with me?

'He hates Germans,' was Rolf's excuse. 'There was no other room they could put him in.' Then he came to the point. He told me Hamdy was an important member of a West Berlin escape group. According to Rolf, Hamdy knew the identity of persons living in the GDR who were members of this group. The long and short of it was that Rolf wanted me to pump Hamdy for information. I told Rolf that as a prisoner myself, I was not prepared to play 'stoolie' for him or anyone else.

'*Ein Kommunist Musst alles gegen den Feind machen,*' Rolf told me (a Communist must do everything against the enemy).

'*Springe aus dem Fenster,*' (jump out of the window), I told him. He didn't seem the least upset.

We were to be moved to another room because Hamdy was making too much noise. They would have to move us away from the main stairway. I objected to this, pointing out that I was not creating any disturbance. But Rolf insisted that I should keep Hamdy company. I told him I'd sooner be locked up with a polar bear. As I sat in the interrogation room, the change-over of cells was being made. Outside the new cell, which was in the same corridor as the first cell, I found half a dozen guards. The door was unlocked and opened enough to let me squeeze through. It was like going into the lion's cage. The new cell was narrow, hardly enough room to swing a cat. There was only one window. The beds were positioned parallel to the inside walls with not much floor space between. Hamdy, stripped to the waist, sat on the edge of his bed.

'German swine,' he muttered, as I sat down on the bed opposite.

'How do you feel?' I asked.

'See that?' he said, holding up a bar of soap which he was kneading in his hands. 'I'm going to fix it that they can't look through the spyhole. Then I'm going to smash this cell to bits.'

For lack of anything else to say, I volunteered: 'I'll help you.'

'Will you?' said Hamdy, eagerly.

For a second, I hesitated. 'Of course I will. But let's figure out the best time to do it. I mean, let's wait until there are not so many guards around.'

'Good idea,' said Hamdy. 'Good idea. When's the best time to do it?'

I was going to say Xmas Day, but that might have made him suspicious. 'Saturday night,' I said. 'That's the best time.'

'But this is only Tuesday,' said Hamdy. 'Too long to wait!'

'But that's part of the plan,' I said, my tone conspiratorial. 'Keep quiet between now and Saturday. Lull them into a false sense of security.'

Hamdy's face lit up. 'Sure! That's it. Lull them into a false sense of security.'

Next morning, before breakfast, Hamdy did five hundred press-ups. 'Got to get myself fit for Saturday,' he said.

I wasn't looking forward to Saturday!

Hamdy got to being confidential. He began to tell me things he had been up to in the GDR.

'I don't want to know,' I told him.

'But I trust you.'

I lowered my voice to a whisper: 'There are microphones in the walls.'

He thought about this for a moment. 'I think you're right. We'll get them out on Saturday. We'll smash the walls down.'

What a bloomer I made, telling him there were microphones

in the wall. He started to write on a piece of paper. When he had finished writing, he passed the paper to me. There was a message on it: 'If there are microphones in the walls, then they will know we are going to smash the cell up on Saturday. We'll smash it tonight.'

I picked up the pencil and wrote: 'Make it Friday.'

Back came the paper: '*Tonight*' was underscored.

Why try to delay the inevitable, I thought. I nodded my head in agreement. Hamdy got the bar of soap and began to knead it. I couldn't see the point of sticking soap in the spyhole when all the guards had to do to see into the cell was open the door-flap, but I didn't raise the point.

That night, we got up and dressed. Hamdy tiptoed to the door and pressed the plug of soap into the spyhole. They would have to open the door to get that off.

'Right Pat,' said Hamdy, and his eyes were two large bulbs.

He bent down, grabbed the water pipe where it left the lavatory pan to enter the wall at the back, and heaved. The pipe came through the plaster on the wall but remained attached to the pan. He let go the pipe, bent down, put his arms round the pan and lifted it clean off its concrete base. A lump of the floor was sticking to the base of the pan. The pipe and the pan parted. He moved back a few paces, lifted the pan above his head and threw it at the door. There was a terrific crash and the pan broke into several large pieces. I picked up one of the pieces and went to work on the windows. I smashed the window frame right out so that only the outside bars remained. I'm not so sure if I was having a 'smash up' or trying to escape from Hamdy.

When I turned from the window he had demolished everything; beds, table, chairs and there was a jet of water coming out of the lavatory pipe. He was now digging a hole in the wall with the piece of piping which had broken off. Even the small peep-door was lying wide open.

They turned off the water and didn't open the door for two days. At meal times they handed the food through the door. Eventually, they took Hamdy to a padded cell. I went back to my old cell.

'Where have you been?' said Beatte when I got her on the

105

'telephone'. I gave her a quick rundown of what had happened.

'We heard the noise,' said Beatte. 'It was terrible. Hamdy must be mad.'

For the next couple of days I was alone. Rolf did not send for me. I wondered about this. Then one night the door opened and Hamdy came in. 'They put me in a rubber cell, Pat.' He was sitting on the edge of his bed. 'And they beat me up.' He stood up and stripped to the waist. 'Look,' he said. There was slight bruising about his ribs but it didn't look at all bad.

'Hamdy,' I said. 'I know some British prisons where they would have half killed you and then taken you to court and charged you with assault. How come they put you back with me?' I asked.

'I asked to get back. I told them I'd rather be with you. I like you Pat.' He fell silent like he was thinking about something. Then: 'I've got a plan Pat.' Here we go again, I thought. He told me his plan. He reckoned that if he staged an attempt at suicide, the Commies, anxious to keep in President Nasser's good books, would drop any charges and pack him off back to Cairo.

'That's a good plan,' I told him.

'Will you help me Pat?' he asked.

'Sure,' I said.

'Tonight, when the light goes out I will cut my wrist, and you bang the door and tell the guard.'

'OK,' I said. 'I'll do that.' The guard put out the light.

'Pat,' said Hamdy.

'Yes.'

'I've been thinking it over.'

'Yes.'

'I might not make a good job of it. Will you do it for me? Will you cut my wrist?'

'I'd rather not,' I said. 'Maybe you'd better think of something else.'

'Please Pat. It's not that I'm scared. I want to make sure it's done right. Please Pat.'

I got out of bed. 'Give me the knife,' I said. 'Now give me your hand.'

I put the blade to his wrist and hesitated, to give him the chance to draw back.

'Are you sure you want me to go ahead with this?'

'Yes,' he said. 'Go ahead.'

I cut his wrist. One quick stroke.

'Do it again Pat. Make it look good.'

Again I cut.

'Again Pat,' he said. 'Again.'

I cut a third time.

'Again Pat.'

'Wait a minute,' I said. 'It's a cutting job, not an amputation.'

'OK,' he said. 'OK. Now bang the door.'

The guards rushed in. Even with blood spurting all over the place, he fought for ten full minutes.

It was time to go home. They made me sign a paper declaring I would never discuss what had happened during my stay in the GDR – and offered me compensation for my trouble if I cared to return to collect it. They knew, as I knew, that I would never go back! So all I got for seventeen months behind East German bars was my board and lodging – and the cigarettes and chocolate they gave me as I walked to the Friedrichstrasse checkpoints – Checkpoint Charlie.

'You are a clever man, Herr Meehan,' were their last words.

At least I was lucky to be crossing the Berlin Wall – even if there was only another prison at the other end. Many people have died trying to make the trip, and I now understand why. In the British Sector, a large black car squealed to a stop in front of me. '*Herr Meehan*?' asked one of the men inside. '*Ja*.' '*Kommen Sie mit*.' They were curt and grim faced. A policeman is a policeman, wherever you meet him. They drove me straight to the British Consulate.

10 Chain of suspicion

I was flown back to England, a puzzled and suspicious man. I understand the working of the criminal mind, I suppose, as well as any man alive. But the working of the secret service mind was another matter. Why had the East Germans handed me back to the police? To allay suspicion about my motives for going behind the Curtain, they said. If news of my presence in the East had leaked out, there was some sense in this. But where did the leak come from? Why had they never mentioned Hector? Why had it taken them seventeen months to complete my interrogation on a matter which, I had presumed, would have been of the greatest urgency? And if they did want a spy sprung, wouldn't I have been of much greater value at large in England, rather than behind bars? The chances of my being placed in a prison holding one of their agents was a pretty risky gamble. With my freedom I could have set up my headquarters near any jail chosen as the target. There were many unanswered questions – too many! A chain of suspicion was being forged in my mind, but the links did not seem to join. It would be some time before they would eventually click into place. In the meantime, I was to exchange my interrogators, MI6 taking over from the SD.

The black Mercedes which picked me up at Checkpoint Charlie had taken me straight to the British Consulate in West Berlin. I was ushered into an interview room with one of the consulate staff, an Ulsterman, surely, because of his undisguisable accent. I began to tell him about Beatte Barwich – I hoped that Western pressure might bring about her release – but he seemed only half interested. But his eyes narrowed when I mentioned our method of communication via the plumbing. He left the room and returned a few minutes later with another man.

'Tell us what you just said,' he ordered. I began to repeat the story about Beatte, but he cut me short. 'No, skip that,' said the Irishman, 'tell us how you were able to talk to her.' I repeated my description of the toilet 'telephone'. They exchanged glances.

For some reason the plumbing was significant to them: why, I will never know. Perhaps they could use it in future if any of their agents were unlucky enough to end up in the hands of the SD. But I gathered the impression that they already knew about the system.

I was taken before another man, a plump man with a public-school accent, who asked me to repeat my stories about Beatte and the 'telephone'. Then came the pointed question: 'Why did you go to East Berlin?'

I had rehearsed this with Rolf before I crossed the wall. He had promised the GDR would back me up in any official exchanges on the subject. 'I lost my passport in Frankfurt. I knew that if it was handed in, the police would be down on me like a ton of bricks. I was on the run, don't forget – East Germany was the nearest escape route.' They wasted no time in providing me with an emergency passport, and I was flown back to London. That night, I found myself in the chokey – the punishment cells – at Wandsworth prison.

It was the following day when I picked up the final scrap of information that would *eventually* make my chain of suspicion fit together – a piece of information so startling that at the time it threw me into a state of confusion. I was told by a fellow prisoner that Joe, the man I had sprung from Nottingham and told to wait for me in Glasgow, had eventually grown tired of sitting around and had returned to London with a Glaswegian. Back in The Smoke, they had been picked up by the police and charged with possessing house-breaking implements. They spent a week on remand in Brixton prison before going back before Lambeth magistrates court. The Glaswegian was jailed. But Joe was fined a mere twenty-five pounds and released. Yet he was a man on the run from a ten year prison sentence! It's impossible, I thought. Even the English courts couldn't make that sort of blunder. I decided that the prisoners' grapevine, normally so accurate, had gone awry this time.

A couple of days later, I received my first call from the secret service. 'I don't want to see anyone – and you can't make me,' I told the warder. Unlike the GDR Britain has strict rules which mean a prisoner cannot be forced to see the police – or anyone else, for that matter – unless he is about to be charged with an offence. My cell door opened again, and in came the prison Governor and his chief officer.

'These are not detectives,' said the Governor, 'they are what the books call the "Secret Service". You must see them.'

'There's no "must" about it,' I replied, tartly. 'You cannot force me – and you know it.'

They left looking none too pleased. Two days later, MI6 – if they still use that title – changed their tactics. I was told that the police had arrived to lay charges against me. I had no choice this time but, of course, they weren't police officers.

There were two of them, one considerably taller than the other, and he seemed to be the boss. He sat me down at a trestle table, and sat on the bench next to me. He produced a piece of paper from a bulky file. It was a photostat of a letter and the envelope in which it had been posted. 'We have a letter here from one of your pals,' he said. 'Someone who decided he didn't want to sign his name.' He held up the photostat briefly. In that fraction of a second, I was able to pick out two names from the letter: Meehan and Lonsdale. I also caught the address of the envelope: The United States Embassy, Grosvenor Square, London. What the hell was all this about?

I played for time: 'I was told you came to charge me with some offence. I don't want to talk about anything else.' He shot a bored look at his colleague and, in the voice of an irritated adult addressing a fractious child, began to charge me with attempting to obtain a forged passport – the follow-up to the ludicrous incident at Petty France when my friend had spelled civil servant with a 'c'.

So they know about that too, I noted; but I was not particularly interested. As he droned on, I was trying to pick up the postmark on the copied envelope. Was it the 2nd or 12th month of 1963? I couldn't quite make it out. If it was the 2nd month, then the letter – if it had been sent at all – was sent before I went to East Berlin. If it was the 12th month, then the letter had been sent after I went there. He had not bothered to caution me before reading the charge, nor did he bother to write down my reply. I had had enough. I called to the screw at the door: 'These men came here to charge me, and they've done it. I don't want to speak to them any more.' The screw, highly embarrassed, knew he must enforce the rules and prepared to take me back to my cell. I permitted myself a little smile at my two interrogators: they were clearly not amused. In fairness, I should admit that it was not behaviour I could have exhibited in East Berlin.

The letter gave me more food for thought. If someone had wanted to betray me, why write to the American Embassy? Why not Scotland Yard? And if the letter had been written at the time of the postmark – I could see no reason for such an elaborate *forgery* – no one in Britain knew that I was planning to go to East Berlin. No one, that is, except Hector! Once again that name cropped up. Once again, I felt a surge of anger at my own stupidity. In a life of calculated risk, I had set about on my most foolhardy escapade on the basis of a few outrageous hints from a man I knew absolutely nothing about. Why hadn't I told him to 'get stuffed' and gone about my simple, straightforward life as an 'honest' crook? Being a man who prefers to take an active role in life, rather than wait for other people to ask the questions, I asked a prisoner who was due to be released if he would go to the American Embassy and ask them if they had received an anonymous letter I had written in 1963. It was a very long shot, but I couldn't think of anywhere else to point the gun. I hoped that the prisoner's enquiry would be so unexpected that it might catch some junior clerk on the hop: criminals can be quite expert at getting at the truth of the matter, not by listening to what a man says, but by watching how he lies! It came to nothing. The ex-con sent back word that the Embassy seemed totally baffled by the enquiry.

As my battles of wits with the secret service went on, I also had to contend with the normal judicial authorities. Two weeks after my return from Berlin, I was taken before the visiting magistrates charged with escaping from Nottingham. I was stripped of 180 days remission, and sentenced to nine days on a bread-and-water diet, plus twenty-eight days in solitary confinement.

I used the time to write a couple of letters: one to Beatte Barwich's mother in Munich, and the second to a girl called Bärbel whose home address was in East Berlin – she was another of my toilet-telephone confidantes. At the same time, I wrote a petition to the British Home Secretary, asking if the time I had spent in East Berlin could be included as part of my Nottingham sentence: after all, I had been behind bars, but this time to the advantage of the British taxpayers – the Communists picked up my bills!

My solitary over, it was time to take up my duties in the 'security shop' – sewing coal sacks with other high-risk prisoners under the ever-watchful eyes of Wandsworth's toughest screws. There is an accepted custom about the 'security shop', acceptable to both sides of our particular society. It is that a man can sit next to whichever prisoner he chooses as a 'mate'. It gives the prisoner some comfort, of course, but the main advantage goes to the screws – it prevents the fights when two guys who hate each other are sat side-by-side. As I walked into the shop that morning, I was pleased to see several familiar faces (ours is a very small world). One of them nodded to a vacant chair next to him. No sooner had I sat down when the officer in charge ordered me to my feet and pointed to a chair across the room, next to a complete stranger. It was highly unusual – but my puzzlement did not last long. Within a couple of days, this man – who said he was serving nine months, a very short sentence for a high-security prisoner – had expressed Communist sympathies, confided that he planned to escape to East Germany – and then capped it all by beginning to talk to me in fluent German. At least the SD had been a bit more subtle with their 'plants'.

He regularly brought up the name of George Blake in our 'conversations' – although that is hardly a correct description of our dialogue, because mainly he talked and I listened. It was an interesting little game, like mental chess. I played him along with little tit-bits of information, just to keep it going. Any mental stimulation must be seized on in prison, however dangerous. One day, we were discussing a regular prison 'grouse' in England, the constant shortage of matches. In Scotland, prisoners are allowed cigarette lighters. In England, they can only buy matches, precious possessions, which are split down the middle four times with the careful use of a razorblade.

'I had a lighter in East Berlin,' I told my *Spitzel* friend. 'But my interpreter took a fancy to it so I gave it to him when I left.'

If my spy took any interest in the remark, he did not show it.

*

My stay in Wandsworth was not long. About two weeks after my release from solitary, I was transferred to Parkhurst on the Isle of Wight. Few people have escaped from the island. One of them was due to make my life particularly difficult in the years to come, but I paid little attention to him. I was more taken with the repeated requests for an interview with British Intelligence – requests which I just as repeatedly refused. The only incident of note in Parkhurst was the arrival of a prisoner who had been in the security shop at Wandsworth.

'What happened to that strange guy I was forced to sit next to?' I asked.

'Funny that,' said the new arrival. 'As soon as you left, he disappeared.'

For reasons which I was yet to understand, I was transferred yet again – to a modern prison at Blundeston, Suffolk, designed to give the prisoner the maximum amount of freedom within its walls, and the least chances of escaping from them. There I came face to face with Joe, the man who escaped from Nottingham with me. It was a chance to test the 'grapevine'.

'I heard this daft story that you were picked up in London and only fined twenty-five pounds,' I laughed to him.

'If you think that is daft, Paddy,' he said, 'you should hear the real story. I was arrested *three* times, and let go every time. If you can understand why, bloody good luck to you. But it's a fucking mystery to me.'

If it was a 'fucking mystery' to Joe, it was an absolute mindbender to me. I had dismissed the grapevine story of his release the first time – his twenty-five pound fine while serving ten years – as a judicial aberration at the best. To learn that the English courts had made the same mistake *three times* was inexplicable. Once again I asked, what the bloody hell is going on?

Blundeston was a good nick, if there can be such a thing from a prisoner's point of view. It didn't serve whisky, and there were no women, so I was bound to hate it. But it had been designed to overcome the degradation of the Victorian prisons which are part of the British system: the smell, the cold, the damp. It had also drawn some of the more enlightened staff, including a fair Governor by the name of Eric Towndrow. But Mr Towndrow and I could not settle to a 'normal' relationship because he kept asking me to agree to an interview with the Secret Service. He made the request because it was his job. I refused because that was my character; the years had taught me never to do favours for policemen, whatever particular uniform they wore.

I don't know who decided upon the final change of tactics, but the change was unanswerable. British Intelligence, explained Mr Towndrow, wanted to trace the whereabouts of 'certain people' missing behind the iron curtain. Perhaps my experience behind the East Berlin wall might help? It was blackmail, of course, but what could I do? If those 'certain people' were prisoners, they needed every help they could get – and my sympathies always lie with the prisoner. I said Yes.

He said his name was Sanders, and it seemed appropriate: he could have been George Sanders playing one of his archetypal roles as the suave, well-dressed Englishman, fighting the enemy hordes with nothing more than a Savile Row suit and a cut-glass accent. As I have always suspected about his type of Englishman, his appearance was smooth but his tactics were decidedly rough.

'You have nothing to fear,' he said as he slipped a piece of paper across the table, 'just sign that.' It was a copy of the Official Secrets Act. It said I could face two years in jail if I revealed the contents of the conversation that was to follow. It also described me as an 'employee' of the British Government. I refused to sign.

'It won't make any difference,' he said, unruffled. 'You will still be in trouble if you don't keep your mouth shut.'

Then we really started.

'What happened over there?' he asked.

Alarm bells were ringing. This guy knew his stuff. He wasn't going to beat hell out of me if I gave the wrong answers and that, in a contradictory sort of way, was unsettling: I have no fear of a man who has to resort to violence to get his way, because that is a show of ultimate weakness. Here was the most formidable opponent of all, cold, unemotional intelligence needling out weaknesses of the brain, not the body.

I told him my story: I had fled to East Germany because I had lost my passport and knew I would be handed back to the British police.

'Cut out the kiddology,' he drawled. 'You went over there to volunteer your services. You wanted to spring one of their agents from one of our jails.' I decided I would tell him everything except my one little trump card: the existence of Hector. Why? Because my views on Hector had undergone a dramatic change. Of all the possibilities raised by our meetings, the least likely solution to the Hector riddle was now the obvious one. I no longer believed that Hector was a KGB agent. In fact, I had decided the opposite. But it was a decision which I was unprepared to relate to Sanders. I told him about my questioning in East Berlin. I told him of all the essays I had written about the weaknesses of the English jail system. I told him about my views on the ease of smuggling two-way radios into prison, about the vulnerability of cast-iron window casements used to house mild steel bars. Did they talk about Lonsdale, he asked, or about Blake or the Krogers or Vassall?

'Vassall was never mentioned,' I replied. 'But as for the others – Yes, they were mentioned a few times. It was casual the way they mentioned them, but they did seem quite interested in Blake and the Krogers.'

He marked these points without comment or particular interest, and then returned to the attack. Who suggested I should go to East Germany? Who gave me the idea of springing a Communist spy? It was all my own idea, I said. It may have been a natural extension of my membership of the Communist Party and my friendship with Peter, the shipyard Communist who had been such a big influence on my early thinking. This was not meant as a betrayal of Peter. As a publicly committed member of the Communist Party, I reasoned that my remarks could do him no harm – if the Special Branch did not know about him and his views by this time, they were even more dim-witted than I thought possible. It was part of my in-built interrogation technique: tell them what they already know.

'What agents do you think they are likely to spring?' he asked.

'How do I know?' I answered. 'All I know is that they seemed interested in Blake and the Krogers.' I had been on the defensive long enough. 'I did tip-off the Americans, you know,' I said. 'I wrote to the American Embassy.'

He smiled cynically: 'You really are a bit of a comedian, aren't you?'

I wanted to sound him out on the mysterious letter. He was giving nothing away. As he packed up his files, he asked off-handedly: 'Did you get all your property back when you left Berlin?'

'Yes – everything,' I answered.

'Are you quite sure?' he asked, pointedly.

I remembered the cigarette lighter. I told him the story and he made a show of writing down my reply. He knew all about it, of that I'll swear.

What few remaining doubts I had were dispelled by the Sanders interview. It had taken some years of thought but, of course, I had been presented with a lot of time to think. The chain of suspicion snapped together. Hector was not a KGB agent as I had believed: he was a member of the British Secret Service!

That was a statement so outrageous, so far-reaching in its implications, that it needed a great deal of justification. Yet it was the only logical answer to the series of otherwise inexplicable events that had occurred since my fatal meeting with Hector after changing MacTampson's infernal £100 note at Glasgow GPO. I went over the links in the chain one by one. How, for instance, did Hector know that I was going to the GPO that day? It is hardly a place I spend a lot of my time. He could, of course, have followed me from the hospital where I had visited Teddy Martin – the hospital was a logical place for me to visit that day. Or had the nurse who hovered so close to Teddy's bed heard my remark about going to the post office – and passed it on? Then there were the two unexplained tip-offs in London, which led, first to the arrest of Teddy at the Westminster Bank, and then to mine in the Co-op raid. If the tip-offs came from Sheila, and I have no doubt they did, how could Scotland Yard have planted an informant in my circle? The only person who knew my where-abouts in London was – that name again – Hector. I had given him Billy's phone number. Was I to believe that if Hector were a KGB agent, he would have contacts in Scotland Yard? It was

116

possible, of course, but it would have been so much easier if he were with MI6.

Then there was my sudden 'promotion' at Nottingham from top-security prisoner to red-band 'trusty', virtually thrown out onto the pavement to work unguarded outside the prison walls. Even the Governor had been amazed by this decision – and quite rightly so. In all the years of my dubious career as a criminal, I have never heard of a PD convict with a series of prison escapes and attempted escapes behind him being given such an opportunity. I can only believe that this order came from high up in the Home Office. Why?

The clincher, although I didn't recognize it at the time, was the incredible treatment of Joe, a man on the run from a ten-year prison sentence who was arrested and released with a minor fine, not just once, *but three times*. I cannot imagine even the world's most inefficient penal system – and England's certainly isn't that – making a series of blunders like that. The only answer seemed to be that someone, somewhere, and presumably someone very high up – actions like these could not be 'rigged' by a filing clerk – wanted both Joe and myself at large. Why?

Again, there seemed only one answer: because they wanted me to go ahead with my plan to 'spring' a Communist agent, and surmised that I had taken Joe along as a potential accomplice. And who knew of my plans for the Great Red Escape? Only one man: inevitably, Hector! I finally came to this decision after my long interview with Sanders. Throughout our talk, I had the impression that Sanders was less interested in what had happened to me in East Germany than in what caused me to take the trip in the first place. Was he, in fact, trying to decide if I was a danger to one of his own men – Hector? Or was he more worried about the possibility of my 'spilling the beans' of some secret service plot that was underway? I will never know the answer to that, of course, but one unexpected thing did happen following the interview: the Home Secretary agreed to count eight of the months I had spent behind the Curtain towards my current sentence. I was pleased, of course, and not a little surprised. I had started to petition the Home Office more out of a need to tax my brains on some problem, rather than with any real hope of success.

When I had finally and laboriously fitted the links of my chain

117

of suspicion into place, there remained only one area for thought: what possible motive could the British Secret Service have had for wanting an enemy agent sprung? I came to the conclusion that in the murky world of international politics, the presence of Communist spies in British prisons had become a grave embarrassment to the British Government.

Perhaps their sentences stood in the way of some new agreements between Russia and the West to move towards détente? Perhaps the Russians were making release a condition of some secret international agreement?

Such questions, by this time, were largely irrelevant anyway. Lonsdale had already been released while I was still in East Germany – I had after all met him face to face. He was exchanged for the British spy Greville Wynne. The Krogers were to be swapped for the hapless Gerald Brooke, a London lecturer who had been sentenced to five years in a Russian labour camp for the trivial offence of handing out propaganda leaflets. The Lonsdale-Wynne exchange, when I eventually heard the full details back in England, finally convinced me that my trip to the East had been a complete waste of time. I had been a puppet in some elaborate plan which was never to be put into action – the puppet master had decided to pull another, more direct, string. I didn't like the idea of being a puppet, particularly for the British Government, but I knew there was little I could do about it – I had been swimming way out of my depth, and I was glad to be back in my familiar shallows, even if I was behind bars.

I decided to forget the entire sorry episode and concentrate on the only positive result to arise from it, my knowledge of the German language. I became a jailbird language student.

11 A spy is sprung

My decision to become a model prisoner, devoting my mind to the pursuit of knowledge rather than escape attempts, allowed me the first peace of mind I had known for years. It lasted about eighteen months.

In October 1966, I was transferred from Blundeston to Edinburgh prison for 'prison visits'. One of the more humane rules of the British penal system allows Scots in English prisons to make short transfers 'over the border' so that relatives and friends can visit them without making long and expensive journeys south. I was reasonably content that night in my cell, listening to the BBC on my transistor radio. The newsflash smashed my cosy, if lonely, little world into a million pieces. George Blake, the British traitor who spied for the Russians, had escaped from Wormwood Scrubs prison, London. The bastards, I thought, the rotten double-dealing bastards. I didn't know who I was cursing – the British Secret Service, for setting me up in the first place, or the KGB for tossing me back to my fate after months of picking my brains. I just knew I was angry with Them – authority as a whole, of whatever nationality or political persuasion. I knew, too, that the escape of a man I had never met from a prison some 400 miles away was going to cause me a whole lot of trouble. It didn't take long to start. Blake escaped on the night of Saturday October 22nd. On the morning of Monday October 24th, two screws came to the main workshop and escorted me back to my cell in D block.

'What have you been up to then?' one of them asked.

'I don't know,' I replied. 'Where are you taking me?'

'The Governor says you've got to go into solitary.'

This was strictly against the rules, because I had committed no offence against prison regulations. When the Governor came to see me later that day, I demanded to know why I was being punished. His orders, he said, came direct from the Scottish Home Department.

'I don't know what it's all about,' he admitted in a puzzled tone. 'I was hoping you could tell me.'

That night, two extra officers were drafted in, one to sit outside my door, one to stay under my window. Someone was very anxious I would not go over the wall. The screw who brought in my breakfast said: 'This is all very strange – do you think it's got anything to do with that spy escaping?'

There was no doubt whatsoever in my mind, particularly when two days later I set out, under heavy escort, on the way to London and Pentonville prison.

Were they 'setting me up'? was the question on my mind. Do they want to put me away for a very long time to keep my mouth shut about what I know? The idea of going back to England worried me, for there – unlike Scotland – they had a 'conspiracy' charge which carried no maximum sentence. If I were to be 'stitched' – framed – on a charge of conspiring to free Blake, I could end up serving the rest of Blake's sentence for him – all thirty-seven years of it. My reaction, as always, was to get my piece in first. The only people who would take interest in my case, I thought, would be the Press. I could expect very little sympathy from the authorities.

My little convoy stopped for the night at Durham jail, and there I persuaded another prisoner to smuggle out a letter to Chapman Pincher, the distinguished defence correspondent of the *Daily Express*. My journey south continued the following day. At Pentonville, the chief officer told me that British Intelligence wanted another interview with me.

'If I have any choice in the matter, then I don't wish to be interviewed by anyone,' I told him.

'You don't want to get on the wrong side of these chaps,' he told me. 'They can be very nasty, you know. Sleep on it and I'll see you again in the morning.'

I didn't take his advice to sleep on it – sleep was the furthest thing from my mind that night. Breakfast time found me still pacing the floor. 'I've decided I don't want to be interviewed by anyone,' I told the chief officer when he sent for me later in the day. The bluff seemed to work. Within a couple of days I was back at Blundeston where a letter from Chapman Pincher was waiting for me. The letter from Pincher was signed 'Chappers'

120

and bore an address in Ewhurst, Surrey. It contained a request that I send a visitor's pass. In reply I addressed the enclosed visitor's pass to Mr C. Pinker. Soon after, Chapman Pincher called to visit me and we spent two hours talking. As a result of what I said at that interview, an article by Chapman Pincher appeared in the *Daily Express* of December 5th 1966. The article, headed 'My Startling Talk With Prisoner 519', read:

An escaped British prisoner who fled behind the Iron Curtain and returned, warned the security authorities that Communists intended to rescue George Blake, the Russian spy, from Wormwood Scrubs.

This was disclosed when 38-year-old Patrick Meehan (Prisoner 519) told me the full story in Blundeston prison, near Lowestoft, five days ago.

I have since confirmed that Meehan was interrogated in February last year by a senior Security official who reported the warning in writing to the Director General of the Security Service.

I have also been assured that the warning was then passed to the Home Office.

Yet no further restrictions were placed on Blake, whose escape was organised by some outside agency six weeks ago.

This disclosure creates a difficult situation for Mr Roy Jenkins, the Home Secretary, who assured Parliament a month ago that 'no allegations relating to a Blake escape were discovered by the authorities' while Labour has been in office.

WARNING
Mr Enoch Powell, the Shadow Defence Minister, is to question Mr Jenkins about Meehan's warning this week.

Meehan, whom I interviewed for two and a half hours, gave me the same information he told the security official who was introduced to him as 'Mr Sanders'.

He claims he is entitled to do this because he refused Mr Sanders' invitation to sign an Official Secrets document which would have sealed his lips on the interrogation.

He said that he was approached by a well known British Communist, whom he named, in 1955 after he had organised the escape of Edward Martin, a dangerous criminal, from Peterhead jail.

It was casually suggested then that Meehan might be useful in rescuing Communist prisoners like Dr Klaus Fuchs, who were in British jails, but nothing further happened.

In August 1963, Meehan, who was serving eight years for attempted robbery, escaped from Nottingham prison, picked up his passport and flew to Dublin. He then flew on to Frankfurt in West Germany, crossed the border near Marienborn and contacted the East German security authorities.

He claims that his purpose was to get money from the Communists by planning and later organising the escape of any British prisoners in whom they were interested.

He assured them he could arrange any escape from any British prison through the experience and contacts gained during his criminal life.

SPY RING

The Communists told him they were interested in rescuing only three prisoners: Blake, who was serving forty-two years for being a double agent, and Helen and Peter Kroger, the Navy secrets spies.

They told him they had their own arrangement for Gordon Lonsdale, the Soviet spy master of a Navy secrets ring. This turned out to be the exchange for Greville Wynne, the British businessman held by the Russians.

Meehan, who speaks and writes German so well that he is taking the 'A' level examination in it in the New Year, was held for sixteen months in *Hohenschoenhausen*, the East Berlin prison used by the East German secret police.

He was repeatedly interrogated by security men and agents planted as fellow prisoners. They pumped him about British prisons and escape routes out of the country.

He told them easy ways of getting to Ireland such as by hiding in a van crossing on the ferry at Stranraer but he wanted to return to Britain and carry out the escape himself.

Meehan was taken by air to a secret destination which he believed to have been in Russia and questioned again.

In December 1964 the Communists decided he was of no further use to them.

He was taken through Checkpoint Charlie in Berlin and handed to the West German police who passed him to the British.

He was then flown to London and put in Wandsworth prison before being sent to Parkhurst and later to Blundeston.

During his stay in Wandsworth a British agent, masquerading as a prisoner, tried to question him but he resisted full interrogation until he saw 'Mr Sanders' who took copious notes and made a full report of the interview.

Soon afterwards Meehan was told he had been granted eight months remission of sentence which he believes to be a reward for the services rendered.

Meehan says he knows the Communists would not be directly involved in the escape of Blake but would engage someone else to carry it out.

IN TOUCH
He showed me letters he has recently received from East Germany from contacts made while in prison behind the Iron Curtain. He believes that at least one of them is a Communist agent keeping in touch.

Mr Enoch Powell is, therefore, also asking Mr Jenkins why any prisoners are allowed to correspond in German with East Germans. Meehan who has used the aliases Meechan and Carson is not seeking money for these disclosures.

His purpose in making a statement seems to be the hope of securing further remission of his sentence because his warning has now been proved correct.

The interview took place under difficult circumstances: a prison visiting room is not the best place for highly complex conversations at the best of times. Ever watchful screws tend to pounce if they think the talk is getting too deep – how are they to know what plots are being hatched? And Pincher, of course, visited me as an everyday friend – the staff would have run amok if they had guessed I was being interviewed by one of Fleet Street's most famous writers.

As a result of the difficulty of our exchanges, there were some minor inaccuracies in the *Daily Express* story. I did not claim that the Home Office had given me remission as a reward for my warning about Communist interest in Blake, although that may have been a logical conclusion to Pincher. I did not say that the girls I wrote to in Germany were agents – I only mentioned this correspondence as a piece of back-up information to corroborate a story which, I realized only too well, must have sounded pretty far fetched. But the lines which, to me, confirmed Pincher's reputation as a noted 'digger' for the facts were the ones which read:

I have since confirmed that Meehan was interrogated in February last year by a senior Security official, who reported the warning in writing to the Director General of the Security Service . . . I have also been assured that the warning was then passed to the Home Office . . . Yet no further restrictions were placed on Blake whose escape was organised by some outside agency six weeks ago.

Not surprisingly, the balloon went up. As I have already said, there had been serious debates on the possibility of the continuing security scandals bringing down the Government. Pincher's article fanned flames which were already blazing furiously. Lord Mountbatten, the member of the Royal Family who became a distinguished sailor, was already heading an enquiry into prison security, Enoch Powell was on the warpath in the House of Commons, and I was stuck in a cell, the most unpopular prisoner in Britain.

A prisoner who smuggles out a letter complaining about the food is considered an unforgivable traitor by the average warder. A man who causes a row on the floor of the House of Commons and goes as far as to embarrass a member of the Royal Family is . . . well, unspeakable. My crime was so great that they did not know what to do with me. So they just left me alone. Or so I thought at the time. With hindsight, I now believe that it was this incident that settled my future. It was the time when the chain of suspicion nearly became a noose.

Lord Mountbatten eventually submitted his report on the Blake escape. In it, he totally discredited my story. Paragraphs 66 and 67 read:

The prisoner added in the course of his interrogation by the Security Service, that he gained the firm impression that his interrogators behind the Iron Curtain were not much interested in Blake.

There is, therefore, no evidence that this prisoner who escaped to East Germany warned the Security authorities, as is now alleged, that Communists intended to rescue George Blake from Wormwood Scrubs.

His Lordship and his committee came to these conclusions without interviewing one of the vital witnesses in the case . . . me!

They decided, it would appear, to accept totally the word of 'Mr Sanders' and his department – the department whose activities the committee were supposed to be investigating. For me, it was a curious reversal of the norm. It was as if a judge had directed a jury to pay more attention to the statement of a convicted criminal than that of a policeman with a distinguished career.

I have always held the absolute conviction that the Mount-

124

batten report was a complete 'whitewash'. I don't suppose that the Earl himself decided it should be this way. But I am convinced that the people who put the evidence before him 'rigged' the enquiry so that its decision was a foregone conclusion. That may seem a presumptuous conclusion – what right has a criminal from the backstreets of Glasgow to question a decision by one of the most respected men in the land? Thankfully, I am not alone. Chapman Pincher, who can claim more genuine 'scoops' than almost any other British journalist, had confirmed my story. But more backing was to come as the years passed, some of it from unexpected sources. First there was a book called *The History of the Russian Secret Service* by Richard Deacon, one of the West's greatest authorities on Communist espionage. Discussing the Blake escape and the strange part played in it by Sean Bourke – the wild Irishman who sprung the spy and claims that it was all his idea – Deacon wrote:

The view of the French and the West German Secret Services was that Blake was definitely 'sprung' by the KGB and that Bourke was manipulated as a useful decoy to draw attention away from them. The West Germans, whose Intelligence went into the whole affair in great detail, as they had a special interest in Blake in view of his machinations in their territory, were firmly convinced that Blake was not only rescued by the KGB but that the British Secret Service actually connived the deed. They are emphatic even today that Blake could not have escaped unless there was either some secret deal between the British and the KGB, possibly involving some complicated exchange of personnel which they did not wish to be published, or by somebody knowing about the rescue attempt and creating conditions under which it could be brought off.

Later in the book, Deacon discusses the tactics of spreading 'disinformation' – the sending back of spies deliberately primed with false information calculated to confuse the enemy's intelligence network. Within this context he is even more scathing than I was of the Mountbatten report when he writes:

In the sixties, there was an undoubted conspiracy to allow George Blake to be 'sprung' from Wormwood Scrubs prison. The CIA were convinced from information that reached them that Blake was rescued by the KGB with the connivance of somebody in the British Secret Service . . .

The CIA were angered by what they considered as the singularly unsatisfactory probe into prison security and the escape of Blake by the Mountbatten Commission of Enquiry. They regarded it as pure whitewashing of what was criminal negligence. Later, they offered a large cash reward to British underworld contacts for information on how Blake escaped. This was revealed when Mr Herbert Itkin, a CIA agent, gave evidence in court which helped to convict Mr Carmine de Sapio, former Tammany boss, on bribery charges [NB: this court case caused a major sensation in America at the time although the Blake connection emerged as a side-issue]. Mr Itkin later stated that some of his undercover work included investigating the Blake affair and the infiltration of London gambling casinos by the Mafia. In 1966, he went to London to obtain information on how Blake escaped to the Soviet Union. 'My mission was successful,' he added, 'but exactly how Blake got away is a matter of national security that I cannot talk about.'

When I read this book, my mind went through a series of mental somersaults. Here was a CIA man giving evidence in an American court, talking about the Mafia and – almost off-handedly – about a conspiracy between the KGB and the British Secret Service. Could this really be the twilight world into which I had stumbled, wide-eyed and ignorant, on the pavement outside Glasgow GPO? It seemed beyond belief. Yet here was Deacon quoting sources, not only from the CIA but from the West German and French security networks. This crazy jigsaw puzzle was too much. The final piece that convinced me was Sean Bourke's book about Blake's escape – it convinced me because, paradoxically, the account as a whole was so unconvincing. I found the mystery of how Blake actually left Britain still unexplained and various episodes so guardedly written as to rouse my gravest suspicions. But two facets of the escape itself stopped me in my tracks. Firstly, Blake had a two-way radio in his possession, smuggled into the prison disguised as an ordinary transistor radio! And he forced a window by breaking the cast-iron casement which held the bars! My mind went back to East Berlin and room 344. Here was my plan coming to fruition at someone else's hand. Paddy Meehan, I told myself, you've been conned! It all fell into place with a clarity that seemed blinding. I had been set up, not only by the British Secret Service, but by the KGB as well!

I had been the sucker: the bumptious, over-confident blatherer who had thought that an education won on the streets of the

Gorbals would equip me to take on the university-educated minds – and ice-cold hearts – which pull the world's hidden strings. The British set me up. The Communists did the dirty work. They picked my brains and body clean and threw away the bones. Why did they get Bourke to do the job and not me? Perhaps I was too obvious a choice with my previous prison record. Or was it that I had shown myself too difficult to silence? As they had said to me before they took me to Checkpoint Charlie, 'You are a clever man, Meehan.' Certainly I was too clever for my own good. All I got out of it was free board and lodgings for almost a year and a half, in a style to which I was already too well accustomed.

There was only one grey area left still worthy of thought: why had the spy masters of two powerful nations thought it necessary to involve the likes of me in such an elaborate intrigue? Was it because they wanted to swap Blake but knew Western public opinion would be so outraged by a simple exchange that they had to find a more devious route? This seemed to be the favoured answer of writer Richard Deacon. Or was the logic even more convoluted? Was Blake, in fact, sent back to Moscow by the British to spread 'disinformation', to report false facts he had been deliberately fed by the British during his interrogation. If this were so, it would mean that Blake was being used, either consciously or otherwise, as a *triple* agent for British intelligence, the doublecrosser about to pull off the final triple-cross: conning the people who thought they were his *real* masters, the KGB. This was the answer that appealed to me. Perhaps I came to the conclusion because, by this time, I was so convinced that intrigue was such a normal part of security politics that only the ultimate intrigue would serve any useful purpose. There seemed to be substantial evidence to suggest that my deepest suspicions were correct. The springing of Blake gave the Russians a worldwide propaganda victory. Dozens of newspaper articles, reflecting on this point, pointed out that the KGB could offer their agents the ultimate security: whatever happens to you, we will get you home safe and sound.

Would British security have handed the Reds such a triumph merely to rid themselves of the embarrassment of keeping Blake behind bars? What secret agreement between Russia and Britain could have been so important as to make the British voluntarily submit to such a degrading propaganda defeat? I could think of no satisfactory answer to this incredible question then, nor can I now. More important, none of the newspapers and books which have gone into the question since have ever answered the Blake riddle. From an official point of view, the British Government washed their hands of the entire business after the Mountbatten report. I doubt if the world will ever know the truth behind the remark of CIA agent Herbert Itkin to that American court: 'Exactly how Blake got away is a matter of national security which I cannot talk about.'

One point in this huge labyrinth of conjecture escaped me at the time. If there were a plot to send Blake back to the USSR to spread 'disinformation', its success depended on one essential: the Russians must think his information genuine. Therefore, the KGB could not know that British security was *officially* involved, otherwise they would obviously suspect a 'set-up'. So the intermediary would have to be an 'innocent', a straightforward crook looking for an easy killing. A man, in fact, like Sean Bourke – or Paddy Meehan! We were back full circle, back to Hector outside the Glasgow post office. I had told no one of the existence of Hector. To be fair, I didn't know who he was. But if the Russians knew about Hector, and that the idea of my flight behind the Curtain had been suggested to me by a mysterious outsider, any information taken back by Blake would be suspect.

I believe that this thought occurred to someone else before it occurred to me, someone with the power to pull some long and tangled strings. My smuggled messages to the *Daily Express* had shown that I was a man with the will and ingenuity to make my case known. Had it also shown that I was a man who must be silenced? And in a democratic society without secret police or political prisons, how do you silence a man with the will to speak out? I was to get a long, long time to ponder that one, the biggest unanswered question of them all. But that was in the future.

12 James Griffiths

I was to meet two extraordinary prisoners in Parkhurst as I served out the remainder of that last sentence in England. Both were to cause me a lot of pain. One was a Lancastrian who manufactured the tallest stories I had ever heard, and who was unpopular with the other inmates. His name was James Griffiths, a car thief and burglar, and I paid very little attention to him. He interested me only because of one exploit: he had been one of the very few prisoners who had ever escaped from the Isle of Wight and reached the mainland undetected. Dressed in prison uniform he walked away from an outside working party, jumped on a passing bus to the harbour at Ryde and bought a day-ticket return to Portsmouth. From the ferry, he took a train to London, sharing a compartment with a prison officer and his wife.

'The screw kept looking at my uniform, but never said anything about it,' he would recall.

He was on the run for three months before being picked up again in Scunthorpe, Lincolnshire, for housebreaking, larceny and car theft. He drew another four years on top of the four he was already serving. With that sort of record, Griffiths should have been something of a hero in Parkhurst. But his wildly exaggerated stories, and his contempt for other people's point of view, caused him to be shunned by the other convicts. I talked to him occasionally, more out of sympathy than anything else.

The other meeting was with a much more charismatic figure known as The Butler, who had spent many of his years 'in service' to some of the wealthiest families in Britain. He was a Glaswegian, like me, and a total rogue – the sort of man who would turn his hand to any sort of crime if the opportunity presented itself. His expertise in prison turned on corrupting screws, with a subtle but evil combination of bribery and blackmail. In later years – after the Israeli illusionist became famous – The Butler was to earn the nickname the 'Uri Geller of Parkhurst' – the man who could bend any screw. Sometimes I think he caused trouble just for the sheer hell of it – to keep his hand in, so to speak. One of his more infamous stunts landed me back in the world I was desperately trying to avoid, the highly publicized world of espionage. Somehow, The Butler had managed to get his hands on some of the files concerning the spy Peter Kroger, who was serving his sentence on the Island. Like a fool, I agreed to smuggle them out – I was being allowed a short parole to visit my father, who was dying from cancer in Glasgow. The papers seemed totally innocuous, but The Butler had this idea that they could be sold to the Press for big money. I took them out stuck inside the cover of a German grammar book I was studying.

On my return, the Special Branch were waiting. The Kroger Papers case was about to burst into the newspapers and once again, the name of Patrick Connolly Meehan was to be associated with spies. I kicked myself for my stupidity – hadn't I been through all this before? I denied all knowledge of the papers, and smuggled out word to Betty to destroy them. Betty, who had now decided to take our legal separation to the ultimate step of divorce, was far from pleased to be involved yet again. A strange relationship, ours. Like Liz Taylor and Richard Burton, we were getting divorced but we refused to allow such technicalities to interfere with our life. The Special Branch either believed my story, or could not prove anything against me. A few days later on the 4th August 1968, I stepped to freedom.

There was one last chore to be carried out, one last long-shot to be fired off, before I could close the chapter on the East Berlin affair.

On the day following my release, I presented myself at the American Embassy in Grosvenor Square, London. Had they received any letters from me? I asked the clean-cut young clerk. He disappeared and returned with a file – a very meagre file, I noted. His faintly bored air turned to one of shock as he began to read. I noticed a press cutting with a picture of me.

'I cannot help you,' he said, his face pale, his manner agitated. 'I must ask you to leave the Embassy at once!'

There was no point in arguing with him. I was never going to find out what was in that file, as I will never know what is in the various files gathering dust in the offices of MI6, the East German SD, the KGB and God knows what other spy headquarters throughout the world. I shrugged and left. Well that's that, I thought. A long, mysterious and rather unpleasant episode was over and better forgotten. Later that day I boarded a train for Glasgow in a happy frame of mind. I did not know that the echoes from the *Hohenschoenhausen* and Parkhurst were to sound out for the rest of my life.

It was sad, but as the divorce had just come through, I thought I could not go to Betty's flat. Instead I divided my time between my mother's home in East Kilbride and the flat of my eldest son, Pat, in Glasgow. My father was dying, slowly and bravely, in Hairmyres Hospital close to my mother's place. The family had a visiting rota, so that someone could be near him most of the day. I took him whisky to drink (my mother would have been outraged if she had known) and we quietly enjoyed our little bedside sessions: there was no harm that whisky could do to him, and it helped bring colour to his cheeks and a smile to his lips despite the pain. I had no plans for the future, and had decided not to make any until he faced the inevitable end.

We were not to be left in peace, however. The Prison Aftercare Officer, whose job is to help ex-prisoners, was being particularly attentive – more attentive than I had ever known before on release and, let's face it, I had been released a few times. He kept pestering me to get a fixed address and to take a job. Eventually, he threatened to have me returned to Parkhurst, so with reluctance I became a salesman in Lewis's, a big store on Glasgow's main Argyle Street. His threat to have me returned to jail was a bluff: he had no power in law to do so. But his pestering was becoming irritating, and I took the job to escape. I couldn't help but ask myself: 'Why is this guy taking all this interest?'

Towards the end of November 1968, I called in to see my mother.

'Why didn't you use your key?' she asked as she let me in the door.

'What key? – I haven't got a key,' I replied.

My mother's face clouded with puzzlement. 'That's funny,' she said, 'one of the neighbours said she saw you coming out of the flat a couple of days ago when I was out shopping.'

We checked with the neighbour, a woman who had never met me before. Not knowing what I looked like, although knowing I was back in the area, she had *assumed* the man coming out of the flat was me. My mother was obviously disturbed. She checked the flat thoroughly but nothing had been stolen. The next time she visited the hospital, I searched the flat again – looking, not for something missing, but something *new*. The past few years had made me ultra-cautious. I was looking for a hidden microphone. I found nothing, but the idea of a bug planted somewhere obsessed me. One evening, as I sat staring at the wall, my mother piped up: 'Those flies are getting on your nerves. I'll get a flypaper tomorrow.' It was December and there was not a fly in sight.

Other little mysteries began to happen. One day in Lewis's, an exceptionally attractive and well-dressed woman came to the counter. She spoke to a girl assistant in an accent I immediately recognized. '*Sind Sie Deutsch?*' I asked. We began to talk. Her husband, she explained, was English. It was unusual, I said, for an Englishman and his German wife to be living in Scotland. Her husband was a diplomat, she said. And, for reasons known only to her, she volunteered the rather startling piece of information that his work was very secret. The alarm bells were not loud, but they were ringing. She came back a few days later, and yet again when I was away visiting hospital.

'That foreign woman was in looking for you,' said one of the shopgirls. 'She asked if you still worked here.'

There were two personal events that December; one bad, one good. My father died, relatively peacefully, on December 12th. I was distraught but glad to see an end to his suffering. And I moved in with Betty again; a middle-aged divorced couple enjoying what was virtually a second honeymoon. Betty was a great comfort in the grief of my father's death.

The aftercare officer was still on my back, for I walked out of Lewis's the day my father died, never to return. Aftercare officers do not like unemployed ex-cons – they don't know what they are up to. So I became self-employed, selling – with a nice sense of irony – security 'peep-holes' which I fitted to people's front doors. Business was quite good – I could earn eighty pounds a week, without too much trouble. I cannot claim, however, that I had planned to 'go straight'. Now that I was back with Betty, my dream of the Big One – the Get Out Job – came back. I still yearned for that new life in Australia, with a small, respectable business and no CID men on my tracks. I was waiting for a big bank. One approach that seemed likely came from an old acquaintance called Gus. Would I meet him in the lounge of the air terminal at St Enoch's Square? he asked on the phone to Betty's flat. Sure, I said. Gus was there with a man called Tommy.

'You just missed the CID,' said Tommy. 'He walked out when you came in.'

'That wasn't the CID,' scoffed Gus, 'at least, not now. He's moved – to the Special Branch.'

Another ring from the bells.

I went to the table where the detective had been sitting. He had left half a cup of coffee and a cigarette still burning. He had gone in a hurry. Now it is one thing to be followed by the CID – I'd had years of experience; but the Special Branch, the men who deal with political villains – that was something new, in Glasgow, at least. It raised two questions. Had he been waiting to see if I arrived, as his hurried departure seemed to suggest? In that case, how did he know I was to be there, in that place at that time? Was the phone being tapped? I didn't mention my doubts to Gus and Tommy. Nor did I take them up on their proposition.

I was in the elevator going up to Betty's eighteenth-storey flat when I heard some children in conversation:

'I think he's a detective and he's watching the pub,' said one youngster.

'How can he be watching the pub?' said one of his friends. 'You can't see the pub from the front of the block.'

The kids were discussing a stranger they had seen loitering around the flats. A stranger, it would appear, who was keeping observation on someone or something. On reaching the flat I went on to the verandah. Using a pair of binoculars I scanned the street below, hoping for a sight of the stranger referred to by the children. It was a useless exercise. How was I to know who was a stranger at the flats? I was very much a stranger myself.

133

But soon after this I had reason to believe that the flats were under observation.

One day, as I came out of the elevator, I saw a young man standing at the entrance to the block. At my approach, he turned his back. Instinct told me that he had turned deliberately. I had a car parked nearby, but instead of going to it, I walked along the road towards a block of flats where my mother-in-law lived. After about fifty yards I stopped and looked back. The young man had disappeared. At that moment a small van pulled away from the front of the block and came in my direction. I had a hunch that the van was in some way connected with the young man and as it passed me I took a good look at the driver: in appearance he was nothing like the young man. I made a note of the van number.

A few days later – I was now in the habit of scanning the street from the verandah – I saw the van parked below. I left the flat in search of the young man. He was there all right. And as I approached him he walked away quickly. I did not follow him but returned to the flat where I kept the van under observation. I noted that the driver's compartment of the van was empty and when, a few minutes later, the van drove off, it was obvious that whoever was in the driving seat had been sitting in the rear. It was to be a month or so before I noticed another peculiar incident. This involved the German dollybird who claimed to be the wife of a diplomat.

It was around early Spring 1969, that James Griffiths came to Glasgow. He called at Betty's flat and, finding no one in, slipped a note through the letterbox. The note, scribbled on an empty cigarette packet, read: 'Pat, sorry to miss you. Will phone back later. Jim.' The name Jim rang no bell with me but later, when Griffiths telephoned, his Lancashire accent placed him. He explained that he had obtained my address and phone number from The Butler, whom he had recently visited at Hull prison. A few days after the telephone call the doorbell rang and there he was. While Betty was in the kitchenette preparing a meal for him, we sat in the living room and talked. He had, he said, come to Glasgow to have me introduce him to a fence named Sammy. He had learned about Sammy from The Butler.

'The Butler says you know Sammy well. Will you introduce me to him?' was the way Griffiths put it.

He went on to tell me he was living in Birmingham in a luxury flat and he had a *position* as sales rep with a firm of wholesale jewellers. That was him all over: he didn't have a job, but a position. This, he said, was merely a cover for his main occupation: the theft of valuable antiques from large country houses. He had recently carried out such an operation in the south of England and had a number of articles to dispose of, including an antique clock which – according to Griffiths – was priceless. Hence his reason for wishing to see Sammy. It puzzled me that The Butler should send Griffiths to see Sammy. Sammy, strictly speaking, did not deal in antiques, only in stolen jewellery. One of his other lines was to change stolen money – at a price. I explained this to Griffiths, pointing out that it would be a waste of time to approach Sammy with an antique clock, however valuable. But I would have a word with one or two of my contacts who might be interested.

In the course of the day I introduced Griffiths to a couple of potential buyers. The valuable clock turned out to be not so valuable – it went for a song. That night I allowed him to sleep at the flat and before he left next day he told me he was on the run from the police in England. He did not say why he was on the run, nor did I ask him. Within days he was back in Glasgow. Again I let him use the flat. Within weeks, he had begun to carve himself a new criminal career in Scotland. You had to say that about Jim: when he worked, he really worked. He broke into the home of Mr Michael Noble, former Secretary of State for Scotland, and stole antiques worth tens of thousands. He and an accomplice stole a car in Edinburgh and found a couple of thousand pounds in the boot. And there were the cars themselves: he stole cars like a desperate pensioner shop-lifting packets of tea. They were usually big, fast expensive models, and he stole them as much for fun as for gain. In the end, they became an embarrassment to him – he had seven or eight stashed away in garages all round Glasgow. He took to driving up to Loch Awe, the stupendous Argyll beauty spot, and pushing them over a cliff into hundreds of feet of water.

Not surprisingly, the Scottish Crime Squad were not over-enamoured by the arrival of this cowboy from Rochdale on their stretch of the range. Only a few weeks had passed before Chief Inspector Samuel MacAllister was knocking on Betty's door enquiring about our recent visitor – who had found himself a place to live by this time. Yes, said Betty, he had stayed for a couple of days but she had no idea of his present whereabouts. When Betty broke the news, I telephoned Jim.

'How the hell could they know I was at your flat?' he demanded petulantly. 'And how do they know my name is Griffiths – I have only used the name Douglas here.'

I remembered that a few days earlier he had phoned a doctor in Birmingham from the flat. He had used his real name.

'I've suspected it for some time,' I cursed. 'The buggers are tapping my phone.'

He didn't seem convinced. Even when we arranged a complex code for meeting places we could mention over the phone – number one was a restaurant, number two a pub, number three the air terminal lounge, he would never use them. Within days he rang and asked me to meet him at the air terminal. I wasn't the only one to turn up. After a few minutes, an elegantly-dressed female walked into the bar – the German dollybird. She went through a play of not recognizing me – and then followed up with profuse apologies.

'Forgive me,' she pleaded, her face lighting up like a beacon.

I had just bought her a drink when Griffiths came rushing in. 'We'll have to go – I've left the car in a "No Parking" area,' he said. It wasn't being picked up on a parking ticket that bothered him!

'Must you really go?' she asked, with her big spaniel eyes.

'Sorry – but perhaps we can have a drink some other time.'

'*Das wäre schön,*' she replied. 'That would be lovely.'

In the car, Griffiths remarked: 'That bird fancies you.'

I agreed with him silently. But for what? These coincidental meetings were becoming too big a coincidence for me.

I was planning a visit to Germany, a family holiday for Betty and our youngest son Gary, during which I hoped to visit Inge Schmidt, another of my *Hohenschoenhausen* correspondents, who now lived in Bremen. But I was having difficulty with my passport, which had been seized by the Foreign Office after they flew me back to London from Berlin. 'When you repay the cost of your repatriation,' they said, 'you can have the passport back.'

I had been offering them money for months – but they seemed curiously reluctant to take it. It was the first time I had ever known a Government department anxious about *not* taking a citizen's money. In the end, angered by the delaying tactics at the Glasgow passport office, I drove to London. There – another ghost from the past – I finally received my precious document at the Petty France office. Back in Glasgow, I rang Inge in Germany and said the much-delayed trip could now go ahead. The following day, the Special Branch called: 'If you ever have any plans to visit Germany, let us know before you leave, will you?'

Betty was goggle-eyed when they left.

'Do you know,' she said, 'it wouldn't surprise me if they were tapping our phone. How else could they have known about the trip?' Betty made that decision herself: I had not mentioned my suspicions to her, to avoid causing her extra worry.

My immediate problem was to get a car for the trip. A friend in London had a bargain going reasonably cheap – I had little money to spare – so I decided to drive down to look at it. Then Griffiths turned up and suggested he should accompany me – if we could call off at Scunthorpe on the way to 'do a little business' with a fence he knew there. The fence, who also dealt in cars, might be able to solve my problem. We set off in a hired car – Griffiths thought this was a joke, for he had so many vehicles lying unused that it would have been difficult to decide which to take. But I was far too cautious to be caught driving a stolen car. As it happened, we never reached London. Just before we came to Scotch Corner on the A66 a car driven by a lady overtook us, pulled in sharply, and collided with a car in front. We jolted to a stop. There were several injured, including a young child, whom I nursed, patting her bloodstained face with a handkerchief. There was a lot of blood that day – I helped two or three people – but fortunately, no critical injuries. By the time the ambulances had been and gone, I decided I could not face the trip to London. We turned back, stopped for a drink with some friends at Appleby and eventually split up near Gretna, on the English-Scottish border. Griffiths said he wanted to visit a girl he knew – he would arrange his own transport back. I knew what he meant.

The next time I saw him, he was driving a brand-new Triumph 2000. He had 'acquired' it from an hotel car park. I thought little of it at the time – so many cars came and went with Jim Griffiths that there was little to remark on. I was still trying to solve my own transport worries: I hadn't been able to find a car suitable for the family holiday in Germany.

On June 24th 1969, I put £150 down on a Ford Corsair at the Chequered Flag Garage in London Road, Glasgow, and signed documents to enter in a hire-purchase agreement for the outstanding £475. I drove the car away, as happy as I had been for many years. I was about to give Betty and eight-year-old Gary the first real holiday of their lives. Not much compensation for the pain I had caused them, but better than no compensation at all.

The snag arose a week later. The Chequered Flag Garage rang to say that the finance company had rejected the agreement because I was not a householder. I had to take my bright new acquisition back. It was a sad blow for the family, but an even more bitter blow to my pride. Here was a man who had let tens of thousands of pounds skitter through his fingers, being slapped in the face for a mere £475. That rejected HP agreement was to lead me directly into the most grotesque period of my life. It was also to be the opening shot of the strangest – and perhaps best publicized – legal battle in Scottish judicial history.

13 A drive to Stranraer

James Griffiths was not the sort of criminal I would normally work with. In a flashy sort of way, he could make an entertaining companion. He bought expensive clothes, more for the label than the style, liked good food, and had a penchant for staying at expensive hotels. He spoke to strangers in an affected accent, spinning them wild stories about his father being an army colonel. Occasionally, he would forget himself and break into his natural broad Lancashire, a failing which caused me unending silent amusement. He impressed few people but was too blind to recognize the fact. As a crook, he was also too flashy and, for me, far too dangerous. I could see no point in stealing cars simply to push them into a Highland loch. To take that sort of risk for kicks was, to me, arrant stupidity – particularly as he never took the trouble to wear gloves or wipe away the fingerprints he would leave all over a vehicle. With his record, even to be lifted for car theft would mean a very long stretch. What I did not know, at the time, was that he had no intention of ever being arrested again.

Ludovic Kennedy, in his book *A Presumption of Innocence*, recalls how Griffiths had once appeared on a BBC tv programme called *Out of Harm's Way*, filmed while he was in Gartree prison, near Leicester. He had bragged, even before the television cameras; telling the world he had no intention of going straight. When he was released, he said, his ambition was to make enough money from crime to buy a good life in South America – 'or get buried'. Then with chilling prophecy, he added: 'So if a policeman charged at me shouting, "Stop, stop, stop" and he caught me a blow with that truncheon, if I had a gun in my possession, I would use it.' No, he really wasn't my sort of villain at all.

But that July in 1969, I desperately needed money to buy a car to take the family on their promised holiday to Germany. When the HP company rejected my application for a loan, Griffiths was the only man at hand with a job planned. He, too, had realized the stupidity of tipping cars worth a thousand pounds or more each into Loch Awe. His problem was how to cool 'hot' cars so that they could be sold on the open market. The answer was, as in any bureaucracy, a matter of getting the right papers. In this case, he needed vehicle log-books, blank ones at that, so that his stolen vehicles could be sprayed and doctored to change their appearance and then described in the log-book under their new guise. A log-book waved the magic wand that changed a hot car from underwater scrap iron into hard cash. Jim had discovered that there were several hundred unused log-books in the local motor taxation office at Stranraer, the small harbour-town in Wigtownshire. There may be as many as a thousand, he said excitedly, but the problem was that they were locked away in a safe. The invitation was obvious. The books were worth £100 a time, and he would handle that side of the business. All I had to do was crack the safe. Even by bank standards, £100,000 was a good 'tickle'. I made the worst decision in a lifetime full of bad decisions. I said I would have a 'look-see'.

We set off at 4.30 PM on Saturday July 5th, 1969, driving the Triumph 2000 Griffiths had stolen at Gretna Green. The objective was to 'case' the motor taxation office to see if the job was feasible. It is a drive of eighty-seven miles from Glasgow to Stranraer along the A77, passing through Kilmarnock, Maybole, Girvan and Cairnryan. The route bypasses one of the biggest towns on the way, Ayr. The journey gave us plenty of time to talk, and I stressed time and time again that if I did blow the safe, it would only be as a favour – I was still waiting for the bank which would give me the Out.

'You're right Paddy, but don't worry,' he said. 'We'll find a bank – I've even been stealing car-jacks in case we have to move a safe. But this Stranraer job will be a piece of cake for you, and it will give us enough cash to sit back and wait for the Big One.' I had told him the method for moving large safes with car-jacks a few weeks before. Never a man to put off until tomorrow what he could steal today, Griffiths had already acquired two jacks but we still needed two more.

The journey to Stranraer took about two and a half hours. A few miles from the town Griffiths noted a hotel with a number of cars parked out front. 'We might be able to pick up a couple of car-jacks from there,' he remarked.

At Stranraer, our first stop was at a garage. While the attendant was busy at the petrol pump Griffiths went off to the 'Gents' and I got out to look at a couple of cars displayed for sale in the forecourt. One took my fancy but the attendant, unable to quote the price, advised me to come back when the sales staff was on duty. I took the salesman's phone number, which I noted on the back of a cigarette packet. From the garage Griffiths and I drove to the car park adjoining the Irish Boat terminus on the sea front. While I went off to look over the motor taxation office, Griffiths remained in the car trying to repair a trafficator arm which had broken during the journey. I had difficulty locating the taxation office – I couldn't very well stop someone and ask them directions – and when I did find it I discovered it to be in the same complex as the local rents office. I was no stranger to the rents office; I had visited it in 1955 – just before a friend of mine named John Harvey had blown the safe. But as far as I was concerned the motor taxation office was not my cup of tea – it was not the simple job Griffiths was suggesting.

That evening, my doubts grew even graver. Griffiths and I remained in Stranraer. We visited a restaurant and a couple of pubs. Around 10 PM I phoned Betty to tell her I would be late getting home. 'Where are you, Stranraer?' asked Betty. When I said 'Yes,' she said: 'Garry will be mad if he finds out you went without him.'

It was close to midnight when Griffiths and I left Stranraer and drove to the hotel where he had noted the cars parked out front. It was raining hard. As we approached the hotel we heard the strains of 'God Save The Queen'. 'That's them finishing up for the night,' Griffiths remarked. 'Once the late drinkers leave, they will turn off the lights in the car park. We will have to wait.' And he was right. The area was so well illuminated that it would have been impossible to get near the cars without being seen. About a hundred yards past the hotel there was a cut-in. We parked the Triumph there and made our way back to a disused Ministry of Defence camp opposite the hotel. There we could observe the car park from cover. Around midnight, or a little

141

later, a bus approached from the direction of Stranraer and entered the hotel car park. Over the next half hour or more, people were coming out of the hotel and getting into the bus. Around 12.30 AM the bus drove off in the direction of Stranraer. But the hotel lights remained ablaze.

'I hope the residents are not going to drink all night,' I remarked to Griffiths. In one of the ground floor rooms, to the left of the hotel entrance, we could see the flicker of a tv screen.

'That will be the residents' lounge,' said Griffiths. 'They are probably watching the midnight movie.' Around 1.30 AM three or four men came out, a couple of them carrying some kind of luggage; they got into a car and drove off towards Stranraer. The rain, which had petered to a drizzle soon after we arrived at the hotel, came on hard again. The night was black.

'Let's get to hell out of here,' I said to Griffiths. 'Those lights are never going to be turned down.'

'We've waited this long, we might as well stick it out,' said Griffiths. Then we saw the silhouettes of people come out of the hotel entrance. They began to walk along the road in the direction of Stranraer. One of them was a woman; I could distinguish her footsteps. About a hundred yards along the road the footsteps ceased.

'They must have gone into a house,' said Griffiths.

At that moment a car drove out of the car park, stopped at the house for a second and then moved off towards Stranraer. The hotel was still ablaze with light. We continued to wait.

It was getting close on two o'clock when a man came to the hotel entrance, a large man. The rain had ceased. Suddenly I heard the panting of a dog, a large dog by the sound of it. The panting came closer and I could make out the form of a large alsatian. It came right up to me but much to my relief showed no aggression. I fondled it for a couple of minutes; then the man at the hotel entrance called out and it bounded off towards him. The rain now ceased and the moon came out from behind the clouds. At last the hotel lights dimmed. Griffiths and I moved towards the car park. While I stood at the entrance, Griffiths went in among the cars. I heard him force the door of one then move towards a white mini van parked hard against a side window of the hotel. I saw the courtesy light come on as he forced the door, then

142

the light went out as he removed the bulb. Impatiently I moved towards him.

'Come on, let's get to hell out of here,' I said. We left the car park and walked back towards the spot where we had parked the Triumph.

'There was nothing in the mini but milk cartons,' said Griffiths. 'No sign of any car-jack.'

Unbeknown to us, Griffiths and I were not the only villains abroad on the West Coast of Scotland that night. As we stood miserably in the drizzle waiting for those Saturday night travellers to be away to their beds, a scene of unspeakable savagery was taking place in an expensive bungalow some fifty miles to the north. Abraham Ross, a sixty-seven year old businessman, who had built up a successful bingo business in Paisley came, ironically, from the Gorbals-Jewish background which had played such an important part in my early youth. He and his wife, Rachel, aged seventy-two, were lying in their twin beds asleep at 2 Blackburn Place, when two men rushed into the room. One threw himself on top of Mr Ross, as his wife began screaming. The second intruder fell on her, kneeling on her chest and punching her viciously in the face. Mr Ross struggled with his assailant, who screamed in a Glasgow accent: 'Get this cunt off me, Pat.' Pat – or the man answering to that name – stopped his attack on the woman and began hitting Mr Ross with an iron bar.

The old couple subdued, they were thrown on the floor. A blanket was draped over Mr Ross's face. Every time he tried to remove the blanket, he was hit again – sometimes with a garden tool which the intruders had taken from the Rosses' garage. Eventually, the couple were tied up. At first, Mr Ross bravely denied that he had a safe in the house, but as the beatings became more severe, he told them where to find the keys. All the time, his wife lay moaning, begging the men to call an ambulance. From the safe, they took something like £6,000, coins, jewellery and a misprinted £1 note which could have been of considerable value to a collector. Not satisfied, they ransacked the house, taking more money and travellers cheques from clothing – and even wrenched a gold wrist-watch from the suffering Mrs Ross's arm.

The cold-bloodedness of the assault continued throughout the night, for the intruders had decided to delay their departure until daylight feeling this would be less conspicuous. They helped themselves to Mr Ross's whisky, and sat drinking until daybreak. At one point, Mr Ross thought he heard one of them say: 'They're not here yet, Jimmy.' Long after the dawn broke, they returned to the helpless couple and, as if they could have still posed any threat, tied them even more securely. They left in broad daylight at about six AM.

Mrs Ross, barely conscious, had begged them yet again: 'Please send an ambulance.' One of them snapped: 'Shut up, shut up – we'll send an ambulance. All right?' And they went.

They treated their promise with the contempt they had spent on their elderly victims. On the way back to Glasgow, they did stop – but only to divide the loot. No telephone call was ever made, either to police or ambulance brigade. The Rosses, battered and bleeding, were to lie as they were, trussed like chickens for another twenty-six hours, until their cleaner arrived to start work early on Monday morning. By that time, it was too late. Mrs Ross, her health already weakened by bronchitis, had slipped beyond recovery. She died before hospital authorities could bring back a little strength into her frail body.

The identity of those two men, who called themselves Pat and Jim or Jimmy, with grave consequences for Griffiths and me, was to become an open secret in Glasgow within days – an open secret studiously ignored by police for reasons which they have chosen never to reveal. 'Pat' was Ian Waddell, a thirty year old petty Glasgow villain with convictions for theft, housebreaking and carrying an offensive weapon. 'Jimmy' – I doubt the word Jim was used – was William 'Tank' McGuinness, a hooligan and pub fighter known for the viciousness of his temper. McGuiness was later to die as he had lived – by violence. Waddell was to escape justice completely. They had used false names as I always used false names on a job . . . to confuse anyone who might overhear their conversation. 'Confusion' was hardly an adequate description of what was to follow.

As Griffiths drove the Triumph 2000 back to Glasgow in the early hours of the morning, I pushed back the reclining seat and began to doze. Griffiths, totally incorrigible, stopped at one point to 'look at' a parked Jaguar. That's all he did – look at it. We had a mild argument, as I urged him to drive on. We continued, and again I dozed. I was awakened by Griffiths saying: 'Isn't that a lovely sight, Pat?' We were passing the international airport at Prestwick, its myriad lights bathing the night sky in orange. We drove on, straight into an incident which should have been our lucky break – should have been, that is, if the police had not decided to misinterpret it. In the headlights, we saw the figure of a young girl waving agitatedly. She was obviously in some sort of trouble. We stopped, and the girl, very distressed, babbled out her story.

She and her friend had accepted a lift from two young men in a white Ford car. Without warning, the car had pulled into a lay-by and she had been bundled out. Then the car had sped off immediately with her friend still inside. Would we help? Please would we help? As I have said many times before, professional villains tend to hate rapists only slightly less than they hate child molesters.

'Put your foot down, Jim,' I said to Griffiths. 'Let's see if we can catch the bastards.' We sped along, hitting eighty mph or more, while I tried to calm the girl in the back.

'What's your name?' I asked her.

It was something Burns.

'No friend of Rabbie's?' I joked feebly, hoping to raise her spirits.

As we entered the outskirts of Kilmarnock, a white Ford came into sight. 'I think that's it,' said our passenger.

Any fears we had for the safety of the other girl ceased as we drew close. She was in the back seat, kissing one of the men. She did not seem to be in any danger. Nevertheless, we overtook it and waved it down.

'Ask your friend to get out and come in with us,' I ordered. Both Griffiths and I were ready for trouble, but it did not come. The other girl meekly climbed into the Triumph and we took them both to their respective homes in Kilmarnock, administering a suitable ticking off about the dangers of accepting lifts from strange men. By now the first glimmer of dawn was in the sky.

The news of the Rosses' ordeal broke on the Monday evening, and over the days that followed details of their abominable treatment began to leak into the papers bit by bit. Public outrage began to mount.

'Daddy,' said my daughter Liz, 'perhaps those fellas who threw the girl out of the car were the two who attacked the old couple?'

I pooh-poohed the idea. 'The rats who did that wouldn't be interested in young girls,' I said.

Griffiths had phoned on the Monday night, using our code name of Alistair, saying: 'Imagine us being down there when that was going on.' His second call – at least I thought it was *his* second call – was even more unwise, as I had repeatedly warned him that my phone was tapped. 'It's Alistair,' said the voice. 'Do you think they know about us?'

'Know what?' I asked, puzzled and not a little angry.

'That we were down there – do you think they suspect us?'

I blew my top: 'Are you fucking crazy?'

The voice laughed, and the receiver went dead. Had it really been Griffiths? The voice had sounded strange. I left the flat and hurried to Griffiths' place. He was coming down the stairs.

'Did you phone me half an hour ago?' I demanded.

'No,' he answered, his eyebrows knitted. 'Why?'

'Oh nothing,' I muttered, passing the thing off. 'My son took a call he didn't understand but said it sounded like a man with an English accent.'

It was a time for deep and serious thought. What was going on? Why should anyone make that strange call? Who knew the Alistair call-sign – except the police who, I was certain, were tapping the phone? That night I confided my worst fears to Griffiths.

'Sorry, fella, but this one could be too serious for lies,' I said. 'I've got a funny feeling about that Ayr murder . . . If the cops come round and ask me where I was at the weekend, I'll have to tell them the truth – that I was at Stranraer . . . with you!'

He took it quite well. 'I don't think you have any option,' he agreed.

The papers were still full of the story. A reward was being offered and the police were appealing for information, even anonymous information, from anyone who might have any knowledge of the case.

'You should tell them about those two youths,' Liz began to nag. I considered the proposition. What harm could it do? I decided to use my own telephone, although I would not give my name. If people *were* listening in, they could listen to my story as well – I might as well take what advantage I could of my unwelcome audience. I related my story to Detective Constable Daniel Scott at Ayr Police HQ exactly as it had happened with the exception that 'a friend' had been involved, not me. When I refused to give my name, the detective replied: 'There is a substantial reward being offered in this case.'

'I am not interested in any reward,' I replied, putting down the phone.

I was still without a car and the date of the German holiday was drawing relentlessly nearer. I made a futile trip to Scunthorpe with Griffiths, hoping his contact there could sell me a cheap, legitimate vehicle. On the way back I phoned Betty.

'The police have been here looking for you,' she said. 'They wouldn't say what about.' There was a silence. I could feel her anxiety. Then she went on: 'There was a piece on the television news saying that one of the men in the Ayr murder might be called Pat.'

My heart sank, too, but I put on a cheerful act. They might be still looking for Griffiths – after all, they had called looking for him twice before. 'Let's get to Glasgow as fast as we can and find out what the hell is going on,' I told him. We got home about 9 PM. Betty told me that one of the cops who had called was named Baxter. I telephoned him.

'We want you to give an account of your movements over the weekend,' he said. 'Can you call in at Central Police Office tomorrow?'

I agreed, unhappily. My hopes rose again when Baxter phoned me back next day.

'There's no need for you to come down,' he said. 'Just forget about it.'

There, I thought, they know bloody well that I wasn't capable of such a terrible crime. I was wrong. On July 12th, a Saturday,

147

they came to the flat. I had no choice. I made a detailed statement about my visit to Stranraer with Griffiths – without of course mentioning our reasons! I told them at length about the incident of the two girls and the youths in the white car. After they left I phoned Griffiths.

'I got rid of the car in my favourite loch,' he said.

They came for me at 8 AM on Monday July 14th, six or seven of them hammering on the door of the flat.

'We have a warrant to put you on an identity parade concerning the Ayr murder,' said Detective Chief Inspector Samuel Macallister. 'Have you anything to say?'

'Yes,' I snapped. 'You're a bloody idiot.'

I was still in my pyjamas. Another of the dicks – who I later learned was Detective Superintendent David Struthers, head of Ayrshire CID – snarled: 'Get fucking dressed or we will take you in as you are.'

Betty and my daughter Liz were near to hysterics. They knew it was all an awful mistake. 'Why should I go on an ID parade?' I asked. 'All I did was help two young girls.'

Liz, ironically, had a job at a bank – the best insurance policy that bank ever had, for they knew I would never touch it – and she was due to leave for work. Suddenly, as she went to the door, Struthers snatched her handbag and began searching it. That was too much for me. 'Leave her alone, you Gestapo bastard,' I screamed.

They gathered round me. It was hopeless. They wouldn't even let me shave. The car was driven by another detective whose name I was to learn well – Detective Sergeant John Inglis. At Glasgow's grim Central Police Office, they badgered me about the whereabouts of Griffiths. I refused to say – and demanded the presence of a solicitor for the identification parade. With a show of reluctance, they phoned Mr Peter McCann. The top brass of the CID kept coming and going, firing questions at me like machine guns.

'We know the crime was committed by two men with *Glasgow* accents,' said one of them, Detective Chief Supt Goodall, head of Glasgow CID. 'If you and Griffiths were together that night, it's up to Griffiths to come and clear you. We know he has an English accent.'

It was blackmail, but I refused to submit – they wanted Jim on too many charges. And, to be honest, I did not realize the seriousness of my situation. They were using the Ayr murder as a stick to beat Griffiths with, I thought. As soon as they found the two girls, they would have had to drop any action against me . . . I couldn't possibly have been in two places at once, even the crookedest cop would accept that. The solicitor arrived. Mr McCann explained that he was willing to act for me at the identification parade, but if I were charged with the murder, he would have to drop the case because of a clash of interests – he had business connections with Mr Maurice Miller, MP, then ephew of the murder victim. I accepted without concern. There was no chance of my being charged.

My first nagging thought that something might be wrong came as I was taken to the CID Muster Room, and not the room where ID parades were normally held – I knew that room quite well, of course. There were six witnesses. Of the first five only the two girls, Irene Burns and Isobel Smith picked me out – as one of the men who had gone to their assistance. Why the police had called them I could not understand because, if anything, they were defence witnesses. Irene Burns was very nervous as she approached me.

'That's him,' she said and managed a flicker of a smile.

Then came Isobel Smith, the passenger in the white car we chased. She was very nervous. 'It's all right, pet,' I said. 'Don't worry about it.' Then she too picked me out. Another point for the defence, I thought.

It was the *last* witness who would be crucial, the tiny, distressed figure of an old man who I realized immediately could only be Mr Ross. He walked very unsteadily and had a plaster on his face. He was helped by a police officer who supported his elbow. Mr Ross, of course, had not seen his assailants. But he had heard them. I was standing at number one in the line, the position farthest from the door through which Ross entered. Detective Sergeant John Inglis led him along the line and stopped at me.

Ross asked to hear the words: 'Shut up, shut up. I'll get you an ambulance. All right?' The effect was electrifying. The old man nearly collapsed.

'That's the voice,' he choked. 'I know it. I know it. I don't have to go any further . . .'

My stomach churned, my throat seized solid. This is not really happening, a voice inside me screamed – it really *can't* be happening.

They charged me with murder, as hideous and horrible a murder as I could ever have imagined. That night, they brought an agonized Betty to my cell.

'When Griffiths gets in touch with you, tell him to come in here,' I whispered. 'He won't want to, but he's got to – he's my alibi.'

She nodded hopelessly, the tears welling up in her eyes. After she had left, I had time to brood on the ways of detectives and their methods of gaining a conviction.

There are those, of course, who will stop at nothing to 'stitch' – frame – an innocent man. They are, thankfully, a tiny minority. There are others who, knowing a man guilty but lacking the proof, will plant evidence to get the man jailed. They look upon this, I am sure, as an act in the true interests of justice – merely helping the courts along in their difficult task of sifting the guilty from the innocent. But in all my long and often bitter experience with the police, I had never dreamed that there were men capable of stitching a man on a murder charge. The enormity of such an act was beyond my comprehension. Yet the incomprehensible seemed to be happening – to me, Paddy Meehan, honest villain.

My only hope of vindication seemed to lie within the gift of a wild and unstable Englishman who, by volunteering to come to my assistance, would also be volunteering himself into a very long jail sentence. The picture looked a dark grey. I did not realize that, in fact, it was jet black.

14 I lose a witness – and a case

James Griffiths did his best to help me, within his own curious code of ethics. At Betty's bidding, he volunteered to give a statement to a solicitor, but the solicitor could not be contacted. He tried to make a statement to Mr Ron Belbin, a *News of the World* journalist stationed in Glasgow. But it was Monday, Belbin's one day off, and he couldn't be contacted either. Three times the Englishman telephoned Detective Chief Supt Thomas Goodall in Glasgow, spelling out the alibi. Three times Goodall advised: 'Give yourself up.' In the end, Griffiths did me the most terrible disservice possible, although the cost to himself was even greater. He got himself shot dead. That, however, was the climactic finale of the worst twenty-four hours of my life.

After being charged in Glasgow, I was taken by police van to the cells at Ayr. There, the question was always the same: 'Where is Griffiths? Where is Griffiths?' I was in an indescribable quandary. The worst act any professional villain can commit is to 'grass' on an accomplice. Yet the worst charge any man can face is the charge of murder. My escape from one depended on the commission of the other. What on earth should I do? The decision was tearing me in two halves.

The police had taken my address book from the flat, and were going through its list of houses and telephone numbers. Jim's number was in that book so they would be on to him within hours. If they picked him up without my help, they'd use that against me. My mind was in such a turmoil. Why, if he was my alibi, had I refused to tell the police how to get in touch with him, they would ask? That night, I paced my cell and came to the inevitable conclusion: come morning I'd have to tell them Jim's address. They'd probably have got it from my book anyway. It was a bad start to a day that was to get progressively worse.

First, there was a medical examination by Dr W. Campbell who, as fate would have it, was the Rosses' family doctor. I can only imagine what thoughts were going through his head, but he failed to allow emotion to interfere with professionalism as he went over my body inch by inch looking for signs of a recent struggle. There were none, of course. He took parings from my fingernails for the forensic boys, who would examine them microscopically for any substance which could connect me with the Ross bungalow. I was in the clear on that one as well. Then it was time to appear before the Sheriff Court in – as the poems and folksongs call it – the 'Fair Town of Ayr'. They were far from fair to me that day.

A large crowd had gathered outside the court as I was led from the police van, a blanket covering my head. The crowd surged forward, or so it seemed to me in my darkness, screaming 'Hang Him', 'Shoot Him'. Two of them managed to break through the police cordon to land swinging kicks to my legs. They're going to bloody lynch me, I thought, in a moment of panic; and I think that this was when the real horror of my situation finally registered. Those people really *hate* me, I thought as I stood before the court, oblivious to the proceedings. They don't know that I'm innocent. I must have been very close to a clinical case of shock. It was preposterous, but it was true: there were people who believed that I was capable of murdering an old lady. What would happen if the courts believed it, too?

I was remanded in custody to Barlinnie prison. As I waited to be driven away, they delivered the *coup de grâce*.

'Griffiths is dead,' Struthers told me. 'He committed suicide rather than be arrested.'

'Don't be bloody ridiculous,' I snapped back. 'Griffiths had nothing to do with the murder. Why should he commit suicide?'

He handed me the evening newspaper: 'Read the Stop Press.'

It said that a man called Douglas had shot himself after running amuck with a gun in Glasgow.

The newspapers had the full story the following day. Griffiths, living up to the threat he had made in the fateful television broadcast, had decided to fight his way out. But he had not committed suicide – he died with a police marksman's bullet in his heart. The five detectives who went to 14 Holyrood Crescent on the morning of July 15th were glibly unaware of the reception waiting for them. They did not know that one of the many cars the Englishman had pillaged belonged to a prosperous sportsman. It contained a .12 bore shotgun and a .22 rifle with telescopic sights.

Griffiths was sitting with the shotgun in his lap as they began to smash down the door. Seeing the weapon, the CID men beat a hasty retreat down the stairs; like all British policemen on normal duties, they were unarmed. Griffiths followed behind, blasting away with the shotgun, catching one of them with eighteen pellets. He followed them out into the street, and peppered their squad car. Turning back to the house, he found the front door had slammed shut. Without hesitation, he blasted the lock and ran back to his attic apartment. From the window, he began to spray the street below with shotgun pellets and .22 bullets. Minutes passed as the police were recovering their composure. Calls went out for armed marksmen to be sent in. Uniformed men began sealing off the surrounding streets. A request went out to nearby Army units, asking them to stand-by. But those few minutes had been too long.

I think that, by this time, Jim had gone insane. The wild stories he had told all his life, the bravado he had demonstrated even on television, had suddenly caught up with him. He had become what he had always wanted to be, but had never been before – Britain's answer to John Dillinger and Billy the Kid rolled into one. While the shocked detectives in the street below were organizing their defences, Griffiths slipped out of a back window and ran through the winding backstreets, his weapons still clutched to him, one in each hand. As always, he was looking for a car.

Outside the Grapes bar, commercial traveller James Kerr, 57, was sitting behind the wheel of his Ford Anglia. For him, it had been a normal day – until the barrel of a shotgun slid through his open passenger window and fired. In one way, Mr Kerr was fortunate: he took the blast in his shoulder, rather than his face, for otherwise he could not have survived. Griffiths dragged him from the car, left him bleeding on the pavement, and drove off at high speed. Within minutes, the number of the Anglia had been radioed to every squad car in the city of Glasgow. Even the local taxi drivers were asked to keep a lookout and report in on their radios. Most men would have realized that they didn't stand a chance. But James Griffiths, on that day at least, was not like

153

any other man. A few minutes later he had crashed the stolen car outside the Round Toll bar. If there were any doubts to his insanity up to this point, they were instantly erased. It could have been the Ringo Kid hitching his dusty mount outside a saloon in Dodge City; for he strolled into the bar and, before a staggered clientele, fired two shots into the ceiling.

'I've already shot two men this morning,' he told the landlord Jim Connolly. 'Nobody moves or they've had it . . . Pass me a bottle of brandy and don't mess me about.'

As he took a large swig from the bottle, an elderly newsvendor called William Hughes was sitting at one of the tables wondering, no doubt, if the scene before him was real. Nervously he reached for his own drink. The scene was real – horribly so. His movement startled Griffiths, who let fire. The shot was to be the end of Willy Hughes. Griffiths decided to leave as police converged on the bar. Firing a couple of shots at landlord Connolly, he hijacked a stationary lorry and roared away. An alert policeman commandeered a taxi and set off in pursuit. It ended when Griffiths turned into Kay Street, a cul-de-sac. It was time for the Last Showdown.

Griffiths forced his way into a two-storey tenement. Holed up in the top flat, he began to take pot-shots at people outside. While other police distracted the gunman's attention, Chief Superintendent Callum Finlayson and Sergeant Ian Smith stole into the house and up the stairs. They were armed with standard issue police revolvers. They trapped Griffiths in the flat, but as they looked through the letterbox the Englishman noticed the movement and moved immediately towards the door.

Ludovic Kennedy's book quotes Finlayson:

'It was either Griffiths or myself. I took my revolver and aimed it through the letterbox at his shoulder and fired. We pushed the door open and sprang at him. He fired at us but missed and slumped to his knees. We grappled with him and took the guns from him . . .'

In ninety minutes that morning, James Griffiths had shot thirteen people, killing one, a helpless old man. He went out as he had threatened but no one had believed: with a gun in his hand.

I doubt if he was sorry with his end. I doubt if the police were particularly sorry either – it saved them a lot of trouble in court,

154

and the taxpayers a lot of money. To say that I was sorry would be to understate the case to such an extent as to make the situation meaningless. I was filled with horror at the carnage he had caused. I was filled with wonder that I had mixed with such a man for so long, dismissing his fantasies as harmless daydreams. How could I have been so wrong? But I was also filled with a terrible foreboding. Just as Mr Ross's identification of me had been essential for the prosecution's case, Griffiths' testimony had been vital to the defence. Judged from the normal viewpoint of legal cut-and-thrust, my position was already looking difficult – even though I was quite innocent. It was to change from merely 'difficult' to precarious – and then to damn-nigh impossible as events unfolded, events of which I had neither control nor understanding. The inexplicable was about to be explained – to the general public, at least.

It started in a small way at Barlinnie where, after one night in the hospital wing, I was escorted to a punishment cell. My continued protests – for I was a remand prisoner, not yet convicted of any crime – eventually brought the assistant Governor to my cell.

'I don't know why you should be subjected to this sort of treatment, but we have orders from the Crown Office to hold you in complete isolation,' he said.

The Crown Office is the Edinburgh-based department which supervises the law in Scotland on behalf of the United Kingdom Government in London. It goes without saying that it is supposed to be totally unbiased. But if this strange order that I should be kept in solitary was difficult to understand, a statement issued by the same office that very day – Wednesday July 16th, 1969 – was incomprehensible within the everyday workings of the judicial system. The statement, issued to newspapers and broadcasting networks throughout the country read:

With the death of James Griffiths and the arrest of Patrick Connolly Meehan, the police are no longer interested in anyone else in connection with the crime against Mr and Mrs Ross in Ayr.

By this time, I had engaged in my defence one of the most colourful lawyers in Glasgow: Joseph Beltrami, son of an immigrant Swiss family whose career as a crime solicitor had already become something of a legend. He visited me in jail that night, and discussed what action we could take against the Crown Office statement. Mr Beltrami agreed with me; it seemed hopelessly prejudicial against my chances of a fair trial. Were the politicians now judging guilt, before the courts had time for a hearing? We discussed tactics which, we hoped, would wipe away the smear of the prejudicial statement. I wanted him to seek a High Court order to silence the Crown Office from making further statements – trying me, in fact, in the media. But he was against the idea. It would only attract further attention to the statement, and increase the public's belief that I was in fact guilty. Instead, we decided to apply to the High Court for permission to undergo interrogation under a 'truth drug'. This, perhaps, would tell the people of Scotland that I really had nothing to hide. Mr Beltrami was able to tell me something else before he left.

'I have had several calls at the office saying you are innocent,' he confided. 'The grapevine says the police have made a terrible bloomer. Everyone in the Glasgow underworld says it was Ian Waddell and another man.' At the time, the name meant nothing to me. It was to become an obsession in the months that followed.

What happened to the truth drug idea? I admit that we were flying a kite, but we could think of no other alternative. It was to come to nothing, however.

The High Court flatly rejected the application with a curt slap on the wrist to Mr Beltrami: 'This court has a duty to protect the accused person from the folly of his legal advisers.'

It was a shame, I thought, that the court couldn't also protect prisoners from the folly of the Crown Office.

As is the way of these things, Ian Waddell eventually arrived in Barlinnie on remand for some other crime. I desperately wanted to have a long talk with him, but I was still in isolation. My letters to MPs complaining about my treatment in solitary had been held back – 'If you want to complain, you must petition the Secretary of State,' was the official line – and I knew I must find another way to apply pressure. In the end, it was simple. I asked Betty to write to me saying that she had seen her MP on my behalf and he was about to take action. As all prisoners' mail is read – and I suspect mine was read with greater care than most – I received permission to exercise with other prisoners the same day as I received Betty's letter. It was a bluff – but they were breaking the rules, not me!

The meeting with Waddell took place in the exercise yard at Barlinnie, dwarfed below the towering walls of cell blocks on two sides. He had been living on his nerves and was well aware that he owed me a favour; several of my old chums had volunteered eagerly to 'do him over'. I had said no: what would it achieve? Nevertheless, I still had to chase him round the prison yard until I finally managed to trap him in a corner. I had never met the man before, and he turned out to be much as I expected – a typical Glasgow 'ned'. This term of abuse, used by 'earners' towards the layabouts in the lower crime leagues, fitted him perfectly. Although he was taller than me, and bigger built, he cowered in the corner.

'Ye canna blame me,' he bleated as I stood before him.

'I'm not blaming you,' I said. 'I just want some facts.'

Stupidly, I was still confident that the police case was so weak that I would never go for trial. Had they blindfolded the Rosses? This was vital to me, because I wanted to be sure that Mr Ross knew it was light when his assailants left – because I could prove I was in Kilmarnock before daylight broke.

'No,' he replied. 'We just put a blanket over the old fella's head.'

Did they use the name Pat?

'Yes,' he admitted, unable to look me in the eyes. 'But that was an accident – we didn't mean to involve you. It was just a name we chose.'

Did they use the name Jim?

'No, I don't think so,' he stuttered. 'We used Jimmy – but all Glasgow says that, don't they?'

This was true. Jimmy is a common form of address to strangers in Glasgow. Billy Connolly, the Glasgow comedian, even makes a joke about it on one of his records: 'Heh, Jimmy, what's your name? That's a daft sort of question, isn't it?'

This was useful. I had always called Griffiths Jim. As Mr Ross had said, both intruders had spoken with Glasgow accents, and

Griffiths' was a broad Lancastrian. The 'Jimmy' and 'Pat' co-incidence could be explained away. With that explanation went most of the prosecution case. Or so I thought.

I let Waddell go. He slunk away, hands in pockets, his head bowed. I learned a few days later that my daughter, Liz, had suffered a nervous breakdown as a result of the case.

To say that I had been over optimistic about my prospects sounds, with hindsight, pitiful. I had been wildly, stupidly, out-rageously self-confident. But then again, it was not until the trial began to unfold in Edinburgh's High Court of Judiciary that the extent of the police case against me became clear. The weakness of Mr Ross's identification of my voice, the strength of my alibi, began to mean nothing as, piece by piece, the forensic evidence against me mounted. Somehow, the laboratory boys had man-aged to build a case against me that was virtually unanswerable. How they got that evidence is another matter. For I had certainly not provided it.

My advocates, Nicholas Fairbairn and John Smith, had lodged two special defences. One was the impeachment for in-crimination of Ian Waddell, a curiously Scottish legal gambit, which would prove me innocent by proving Waddell guilty. The second line of defence was my alibi, backed up by the girls in the car chase and evidence from people who had been at the hotel Griffiths and I had watched that fateful night. All the movements I had witnessed in that hotel car park were corroborated by the people who were there. Yet, as history knows, my evidence was not strong enough to match the case put forward by the Solicitor General for Scotland, Mr Ewan Stewart QC, assisted by Mr John McCluskey QC and Mr J. M. Pinkerton – a formidable legal trio.

I will only summarize the prosecution case – because I want to examine it, and its deficiencies, at length later.

Briefly, the jury were told – and chose to believe – the follow-ing:

1 That on my admission, I was in the vicinity of Ayr with James Griffiths that night.
2 Mr Ross had heard the intruders call each other Pat and Jim.

3 Mr Ross's identification of my voice speaking one emotive sentence was positive.

4 A pair of my shoes, taken from my flat after the arrest, were impregnated by bitumen chippings similar to those on the roof of Mr Ross's garage, where the intruders had climbed to cut the bungalow's telephone wires.

5 A pair of trousers, also taken from my flat, had bloodstains in the right hand pocket. They were blood group 'O' – the same as Mr and Mrs Ross.

6 Scraps of paper found in the pocket of a driving coat owned by Griffiths were identical to paper used by Mr Ross to line the drawers of his household safe.

Taken together, this makes a formidable list.

The ritual lasted four days, but after the first two I knew I was doomed. They not only found me guilty of murder. They also said Guilty to stealing the Triumph 2000 with Griffiths – which I did not do. I admitted another charge of trying to help Griffiths obtain a false passport, although the judge insisted on registering a Not-guilty plea. This, the minor charge, thrown in, my counsel were convinced specifically to link me more closely to Griffiths, was the only crime I had in fact committed. Life imprisonment seemed a little severe for signing a false name on a passport form!

15 Verdict on the prosecution

The following morning, I awoke to realize that it hadn't been a terrible nightmare. I opened and closed my eyes several times, but the walls would not go away. I am a *convicted murderer*, I thought with a shudder. How had it happened? What went wrong? Were all those fragments of forensic evidence – the bloodstain, the scrap of paper, the bitumen chippings – just coincidences, clicking together like some devilish jigsaw with two other undeniable strokes of fate: the fact that Jim and I had been driving through Ayrshire that night, and the haphazard decision of Waddell and his accomplice to use the names of Pat and Jimmy. Were they coincidences – or were hidden hands still pulling strings?

In the aftermath of the murder and my arrest, I had forgotten the series of mysterious happenings following my release from Parkhurst. The stranger who entered my mother's flat; the young man and the van parked outside Betty's flat; the Special Branch man who left so hurriedly when I walked into a bar; the German dollybird with the oh-so-secret husband; the tapping of my telephone and my solitary confinement when they first dumped me in Barlinnie. I had forgotten these incidents until another sinister episode jogged my memory.

A few days after my wrongful conviction, Joe Beltrami, whose faith in my innocence was never to waver, called to discuss my appeal. We sat down in the interview room and waited for the warder to leave. Fixedly, he stood his ground, despite bitter protests from both myself and Mr Beltrami.

'I have orders to remain in the room and listen to everything that is said,' he said stolidly.

He obviously meant what he was saying, but the situation was uniquely irregular. Prisoners in Scotland have few rights, but among those which do exist is the *absolute* freedom to discuss their cases with their legal advisers in privacy. It is a right laid down by the law of the land.

'This is highly irregular,' stormed Mr Beltrami. 'No one has the right to give such an order.' He was about to stamp off to see the Governor, but I restrained him with a hand on his arm.

'It doesn't matter,' I said quietly. 'We have nothing to hide. Whatever he reports back can only be to our own good.'

Being a lawyer, Mr Beltrami was enraged because the law was being broken. I was more interested in the pursuit of my case. And, of course, there was nothing the guard could overhear that could be prejudicial – as an innocent man, I could say nothing incriminating. Reluctantly, the solicitor agreed to go on with the interview. He, too, saw the point of my argument. But he could not realize that my suspicions about the guard's presence had little to do with the Ayr murder. I believe he was there to hear anything that was said about more distant happenings – about East Berlin, about Blake, about Hector.

My appeal was a mere formality. It was summarily dismissed on November 25th, 1969. The following day I was driven under heavy escort to that place which seemed like becoming my second home – Peterhead prison. I was to have a long, long time to think about the trial and the 'coincidences' it raised – seven years, in fact. I began by examining the prosecution points one by one . . .

The place
Of course, I had admitted to having driven through the area twice that night, going to and from Stranraer. My main witness was dead, but there were the people at the hotel – who had not seen me, of course, but whose movements I could have only known about because I was there at the time watching. And there were the girls and the youths in the car chase. They could prove that I was in Kilmarnock just before dawn.

The names
Mr Ross testified that the names Pat and Jim were used during the attack – meaning, as the jury accepted, Pat Meehan and Jim Griffiths. Pat is a very common Christian name among Scots Catholics. Jim is not – but was it Jim or was it Jimmy, perhaps the most common greeting of all among Glaswegians? Waddell had already told me that he thought it had been 'Jimmy' – but

for obvious reasons, Waddell would not be prepared to testify to that on my behalf. How could I force this issue?

The identification

Mr Ross was in a very distressed condition when he identified my voice at the ID parade. But one piece of evidence at the trial was nagging at my subconscious. At the trial, two senior police officers had testified that Mr Ross was the *first* witness to view the line up. I knew that he had been the *last*. There must be some significance to this discrepancy, but what was it? Why should the police choose to lie – Mr Ross had identified me, albeit tenuously, so what difference did it make whether he did it before or after the other witnesses?

The bitumen chippings

It was known that bitumen of this type was widely used on buildings all over the country. If there were chips stuck to the soles of my shoes, I could have picked them up almost anywhere – even in Lewis's store in Glasgow! The most likely answer to this puzzle, quite frankly, was that the bitumen had been planted.

The bloodstain

This evidence, in particular, had come as a grave shock to me until I remembered the car accident on the road near Scotch Corner before the murder. I had helped three people who had suffered cuts, including the child whose mouth I wiped with my handkerchief. Had I put the bloody handkerchief into my pocket, so causing the stain? Of course, the stain was said to be group 'O' – the same as the Rosses'. But the court had been told that 'O' was one of the most common groups, shared by tens of thousands of people. There were further tests which could have split the sample into much smaller sub-groups, thus making the evidence far more positive. But the police had not asked for this more detailed examination. Why?

The scraps of paper

This, of the round half-dozen of incredible coincidences, was perhaps the most convenient piece of evidence in the police armoury. James Griffiths was dead, so he could not deny that the paper had ever been in the pocket of his car coat. But there was considerable doubt about the evidence. Mr Ross couldn't remember lining his safe with paper. And there was a time lapse between the murder and the discovery of the paper by forensic experts that the police found difficult to explain.

Just thinking out the questions which needed to be asked took me some months and I had little else to think about. Getting those questions answered was a very different matter. A 20th century Sherlock Holmes, with complete freedom and the full backing of the Establishment, would have found it a difficult case to crack. I was no Sherlock Holmes, not even a Dr Watson; and I was stuck in prison miles away from anywhere on the Aberdeenshire coast. I needed allies – where was I to find them?

I had a good start: Betty, as loyal as ever, was utterly convinced of my innocence. My oldest son, Pat, now twenty-two years old, was prepared to dedicate hours of time and endless youthful zeal to tracking down witnesses whose testimony raised more and more doubts about the case presented by the police. There was Joe Beltrami, the first of a series of solicitors who worked indefatigably – and for little reward – in my interests because they believed that these, too, were the interests of justice. A couple of MPs, Frank McElhone and David Steel, began to take an interest; and the media – press, radio and television – were already picking up the grumbles of outrage from the Glasgow underworld. Every villain on the Clyde knew I was innocent, and so did every crime reporter.

In June 1971, our campaign gained a major ally in the form of Ludovic Kennedy, the broadcaster and writer, whose brilliant book, *10 Rillington Place*, finally cleared the name of the unhappy Timothy Evans, falsely convicted of the murder of his wife. Mrs Evans, in fact, died in a London slum at the hands of Christie, the mass murderer. The Evans family and Christie lived in the same house in Rillington Place – the unhappy Welshman's only 'crime'. Kennedy's book eventually forced a highly reluctant Government to admit that Evans had been wrongly convicted. It did not help Evans all that much, however. He had already been hanged! I had been lucky to escape the same fate. When Kennedy joined the ranks of the people campaigning for my release, I was overjoyed. Only a few more weeks and I'll be free, I thought. Those weeks were to stretch into months and then into years.

While I occupied my time in prison writing letters by the hundred to anyone who had a slight interest in the case, this small but energetic group of helpers began to dissect the case against me fact by fact. One by one, glaring irregularities in the police evidence came to light. Those irregularities can be studied now, taken one by one with the six major points of the Crown case. To read them takes a matter of minutes. It should be remembered that the refutation of the prosecution case took six long years to gather – and was, in fact, only made known to the public by the publication of Kennedy's book in 1976.

Point one My presence in the area with James Griffiths.

I had admitted this quite freely, thinking that my detailed account of my movements that night would show that it was impossible for me to have been at the Rosses' house. In fact, the police seized on the innocent confession of my whereabouts to prove that I had the opportunity of committing the crime. By sending police drivers over the route we had covered, the prosecution alleged that there was a missing thirty minutes in my story – thirty minutes in which Griffiths and I could have committed the burglary and murder. Yet hadn't Mr Ross himself told the court that the intruders stayed there most of the night, taking time to drink most of his whisky? Lord Grant advised the jury to consider the 30-minutes theory – overlooking to mention our ten-minute stop in Ballantrae when Griffiths got out to 'look over' a parked Jaguar. As Kennedy points out in his book, if that stop had been included in the court's timetable, we would have been left with twenty minutes to cut the phone wires, steal tools from the garage, enter the house, attack Mr and Mrs Ross, beat Mr Ross into submission, open the safe, sack the safe, search the house for more loot, drink Mr Ross's whisky, tie the couple even more securely and leave. Even on that schedule, we would have been picking up the distressed Irene Burns seven miles away just eleven or twelve minutes after leaving the bungalow. Would two men who had just committed a serious and brutal robbery stop to pick up a hitch-hiker, however distressed, so soon after leaving the scene of the crime? As Kennedy comments: 'The idea was pure fantasy.'

Point two Pat and Jim.

As I have said before, Pat is a common Glaswegian name, and Jimmy a universal form of address in that city. But was it Jim or Jimmy? In his evidence, Mr Ross said that he had heard the name Jim, which became a major point of the prosecution case. The jury chose to ignore the fact that later in the trial Mr Ross himself invalidated the evidence by saying that both were Scottish voices – and more so they both sounded like *Glasgow* voices. Griffiths was a broad Lancastrian! However the really sinister background to the Jim versus Jimmy conflict was not to emerge until December 1971, when after seven months prodding, the Crown Office produced a copy of a telex message sent out, according to the police, on the day the robbery was discovered. After giving the details of the robbery, the telex went on:

DISCRIPTION (sic) OF MEN:
1 6 FEET, SLIM BUILD REFERRED TO AS 'JIM'.
2 SMALLER THAN NO 1. REFERRED TO AS 'PAT'.

This, despite the spelling mistake, seemed a conclusive piece of evidence. Kennedy admits that 'to my eternal shame, I now had strong doubts – despite all the contrary evidence – about Meehan's innocence.' It was not until a good deal later that this telex was submitted to closer scrutiny. It was shown to an experienced police telex operator who, as Kennedy reports, expressed his 'complete bewilderment' on reading it. Kennedy wrote:

Apart from the spelling mistake, he points out that the message, if genuine, has no address, there is no name or even initials of either the authorizing officer or the transmitting officer, there is no date, and the time of origin is corrupt... The description of Pat as being smaller than 'Jim' is strange, as Mr Ross never saw the second man at all, Kennedy wrote. At this time I felt that the undoubted efforts of Mr Beltrami were nonetheless fruitless, and I decided to take the matter out of his hands and consult a fresh solictor.

My new solicitor, Mr Ross Harper, had written to the Crown Office requesting a copy of the telex in May 1971. After several reminders, he finally received the copy in December.

Point three The identification parade.

Mr Ross's identification of my voice was, of course, one of the main planks of the prosecution case – and even that was shaky. As Mr Ross told defending counsel: 'Well, at the time I was kind of sure, *but I think it must be difficult to recognize a voice.*'

In those first months in prison, I had been increasingly fascinated by an apparent piece of police deceit. They had said Mr Ross was the first to view (or rather listen to) the ID parade. Yet I knew he had been the last. Why had the police chosen to lie? Pat, my son, went tramping round the witnesses and the man who had stood with me at the parade – men whom the police had invited in off the streets on the promise of a small fee for their services. Gradually the truth began to emerge. Fourteen months after my wrongful conviction, Irene Burns made a written statement to Joe Beltrami. It read:

Isobel Smith [the second girl in the white car incident] and I were next asked to take part in an Identification Parade. I remember it well. The first room into which we were put was an office where two or three people were typing. We were transferred to another room in which there were a number of people. Before we moved we were told not to discuss the reason for our presence. We were again moved into a third room. The old man was taken out of the room first. The other people were then called out. I was second last to be called, Isobel last.

I was told to pick out the man who had given me a lift. I picked him out. I did not see Isobel again until she had been to the Identification Parade. When my turn was over, I was put into another room with those people who had taken part in the Identification Parade. The old man asked me if I had picked out anyone. I told him I had but I cannot remember what he said to that. Isobel came in and together we discussed the Parade and I described Mr Meehan to Isobel. The old man was sitting near us as we were talking. Isobel and I both agreed that we had picked out the same person.

The old man then left the room with a nurse, I think. He was the first to leave the room and I did not see him again.

Signed by Irene Burns

On the face of it, this seems a fair description of a properly conducted identity parade. The 'old man' was, of course, Mr Ross and, as he was the prime witness, he had been taken out – *she presumed* – to inspect the line-up first. And, as she says, she was warned not to discuss the reason for her presence there *before she saw the parade*. But I couldn't see why the police had lied at the trial, and even on the day of the parade itself, I had been surprised that it was not staged in the normal room. The answer to the puzzle came as other people made sworn statements, agreeing with me that Mr Ross was not the first witness. The solicitor I had telephoned that day, Mr Peter McCann, wrote:

'I cannot swear that there were no other witnesses after Mr Ross, but I am perfectly satisfied that Mr Ross was not the first witness to enter that room.'

Several others, including men who actually took part in the parade to assist the police, swore that Mr Ross was the *last* witness. So it became obvious that three rooms were in use that day. Mr Ross had been taken from one and into another which was *not* the ID room. There he was joined by the other witnesses after they had seen the parade. The significance for this strange game of room switching lies in Irene Burns' statement: 'The old man asked me if I had picked anyone out . . . I described Mr Meehan to Isobel . . . the old man was sitting near us as we were talking.' For it is now clear beyond doubt that Mr Ross went before that ID parade having already heard the two girls describing me to each other. And he himself had asked Irene Burns if she had picked anyone else out – a prime breach of the rules covering ID parades! The jury had chosen to convict me on Mr Ross's shaky evidence, even after he admitted it was difficult to identify a voice. How would they have reacted if they had known that the parade had been *fixed*?

Point four The bitumen chippings.
Even the prosecution had to admit that these bitumen-covered chippings, said to have been found on a pair of my shoes, were common throughout Scotland. Nevertheless, they pointed out, they were similar to those found on the felt roof covering of Mr Ross's garage. If people were machines, and not fallible humans, the defence could have wiped this point off the slate. One of the few points in my favour on the forensic evidence was that, in my work at Lewis's store in Glasgow, I had actually been in charge of selling identical bitumen-covered felt to do-it-yourself customers. So I had more cause than most to have those chippings

on my shoes. I doubt if the jury accepted this answer: wasn't it, after all, just another coincidence too big to be believed? My attitude – in view of other evidence from the forensic laboratories – was that the chippings had never been there in the first place. As we will see, there was a much more damning piece of 'proof'.

Point five The bloodstain.

The prosecution's efforts in putting this piece of evidence – that the tiny 'O' group stain inside my pocket was the same group as the Rosses' were, if you will forgive the contradiction, noticeably *defensive*. Dr Anthony Grogan, who had taken another blood sample from me at Edinburgh prison, stated that the 'O' blood group was common for 45 per cent of the population – and the figure is even as high as 52 per cent in the West of Scotland. Questioned by the defence, he said that it was possible to divide each blood group into several sub-divisions – in fact, he said, in the near future it might be possible to break down human blood to such an extent as to make a sample as individualistic as a finger print. And although science had not yet reached that stage, he added: 'In paternity cases, I believe it is published [in medical papers] that there is a seven to one chance of eliminating an innocent person on the ABO grouping only.'

The next witness was William Muir, chief technician at the blood transfusion centre which had examined the sample from my pocket. It was, he said, group 'O'. Almost surreptitiously, the Attorney General asked: 'I take it you didn't do any further sub-divisions of Group "O"?' Mr Muir answered with a simple 'No'.

The impact of the testimony from these two witnesses came as a jarring revelation when, weeks after the trial, I mulled over the full transcript in my cell. The court was told that in a simple paternity case – unpleasant, even sordid, perhaps, but hardly tragic – innocent fathers were seven times more likely to be cleared than condemned on a simple forensic test. Yet in a murder trial, no one had bothered to break down a blood grouping common to half the population of Scotland. Why? These tests are ordered by the police. They had chosen not to ask for detailed analysis. Were they afraid, perhaps, that this little piece of evidence – innuendo would be a better word – would *damage* their case, rather than improve it? I had been involved in that car crash near Scotch Corner, where I had helped two or three bleeding people. On Dr Grogan's evidence – given, I repeat, for the *prosecution* – the odds against one of those two or three people *not* having Group 'O' blood would have been very high. I think this attitude towards the blood test – the refusal to discover as much of the truth as was readily available – shows that the police were more interested in convicting me than identifying the real perpetrators of the Ross murder. It wasn't, of course, the greatest wrong done me.

Point six The scraps of paper.
The previous five points were, individually, all arguable in a spirited defence, although together they added up to a formidable indictment. What was needed to ensure my conviction was the clincher – a cast-iron, incontrovertible item of proof. It came in the form of two tiny scraps of paper. Both were old: one was brown, the other white and bearing a few words of small print. It appeared to come from the pages of a diary. Superintendent John Cowie told the court he had seen papers like this lining the drawers in Mr Ross's safe. Detective Inspector Cook, the forensic expert, testified that similar pieces had been found in the pocket of Griffiths' car coat.

'I am of the opinion that they have a common origin,' said Cook in what was probably the most damning line of testimony in the entire trial.

The paper 'proved' that Griffiths had taken items from the safe. Griffiths was 'proved' to have been with me the night of the robbery. Therefore I was 'proved' to have been with Griffiths and was, therefore, *ipso facto*, guilty. It took a long time for the mysterious circumstances surrounding the discovery of those scraps of paper to come to the public eye. I had known this evidence to be unsatisfactory from the moment I heard it given in court. Mr Ross had cast extreme doubt on it by telling the jury that he could not remember lining the safe drawers with paper. The truth, with hindsight, can now speak for itself.

Detective Superintendent Cowie gave the safe a thorough inspection within hours of the robbery being discovered. It was empty, and he swore this was so in a statement of facts made before the trial. The following day, July 8th, Detective Inspector Cook visited the house and made a detailed report of what he had discovered after a minute forensic examination. His report made no mention of scraps of paper from the safe. Later, the safe was removed to Ayr police station as a piece of evidence. It sat there – one would imagine untouched – for six weeks. On August 18th, Cowie returned from his annual leave to meet Mr Struthers, the other leading detective on the case. Struthers revealed that on July 31st Cook had discovered two scraps of paper in Griffiths' car coat pocket. These pieces of information caused Cowie to recall having seen similar bits of paper in the safe the day of the murder. They go to the safe and – well, would you believe it? – there they are, the vital clues overlooked all this time. Hey Presto!

It was at this time that I was told, in my cell at Barlinnie, that the police wanted to take away my suit for a further forensic test. This caused me great concern. It had already been examined once. What were they looking for now? With the help of prison officers – all of whom were convinced of my innocence – I went through the pockets of my suit with a fine tooth comb. They were empty.

'If they plant anything it will have to be something that will only show up under a microscope,' said one of the prison officers. Then the garment was handed over. I had seen it all before. The mysterious appearance of forensic evidence in cases the CID were finding difficult to crack. As it happened, of course, nothing was discovered in my clothing. It was all piled on to the dead and gone – Jim Griffiths. In a way, that made it even more difficult to answer. I have called this chapter 'Verdict on the Prosecution'. My verdict must by now be fairly obvious: I was framed. I hope the reader will come to the same conclusion, for I have tried to present the case, for and against, as fairly as I can. The jury, of course, believed the prosecution – although only by a majority verdict of nine votes to six. My problem was to convince the courts, and finally the Government of the United Kingdom, that the jury had been wrong.

16 Royal Pardon

From the beginning it was obvious that the battle would have to be fought on three fronts. I had three main opponents . . . the law, the politicians, and Ian Waddell.

The law, someone once said, is an ass. I came to look upon it as a mule – bad tempered, intractable and, above all, stubborn. It had made an appalling mistake but, despite its oft repeated high-minded principles, it was to refuse to admit it. The only way to fight the law is with its own weapons. I began to study some of the more obscure areas of the Scottish legal code. Politicians, too, are not given to confessing their own errors readily. Perhaps they feel they are perfect: any hard-pressed voter in the British Isles would tell them differently – except none would listen. Neither are they particularly anxious to carry out their prime duty, which is the protection of the weak. It is difficult to imagine anyone in a weaker position than a convicted 'murderer' locked away in his prison cell; so I knew that this, too, would be an uphill struggle. I had to enlist powerful allies, the media and, in turn, public opinion. Ian Waddell would, on the face of it, be the most difficult target. There were few pressures I could exert on him. My friends outside would happily work him over – some were itching to lay their fists on him – but any threats of physical violence had to be diverted. Any attack on Waddell would automatically be laid at my door, whether I was involved or not – and wasn't I already in enough trouble? (That must rank as one of the understatements of all time!) In the end, Waddell came to my assistance voluntarily in a most remarkable way. Whether it was from avarice, a longing for notoriety or straightforward stupidity is something only he can tell.

During my trial, the defence had called Waddell as a witness to bolster our case of 'incrimination'. Before he was cross-examined, Lord Grant, the judge, warned him that he had no immunity from prosecution should he admit to any crime. It was a warning he took to heart; and he refused to answer some of the earlier questions. The defence did, however, have one piece of concrete evidence against him: that within a few days of the murder, he gave a Glasgow solicitor, Mr Carlin, £200 to defend him should he be questioned in connection with the Ayr murder. Asked if this were true, Waddell replied: 'No.'

'That is a lie . . .' my advocate, Mr Fairbairn, began to say before he was silenced by Lord Grant.

Nevertheless, that one word 'No' was enough to leave a future line of attack. Mr Carlin testified that the £200 had been offered. So Waddell had not avoided the question – as was his right – but he had given an answer. With a lie.

Mr Beltrami had already sent a dossier to the Secretary of State for Scotland, Mr William Ross MP, calling for a review of the case, when Waddell appeared before the High Court in April, 1970, charged with perjury. After some initial haggling, he pleaded guilty. His one word 'No' was considered serious enough to earn him a three year jail sentence. And in a hugely significant comment, the Judge, Lord Cameron, said of Waddell's evidence at my trial: 'Supposing he had told the jury the truth, they might have taken a very different view of an unemployed labourer handing over a substantial sum of money.'

That, I thought, was that.

Lord Cameron seemed to be going as far as he possibly could to say that the verdict in my case had been a mistake. With the backing of one of Scotland's most revered legal figures, I thought, the Secretary of State could not fail to re-open my case. May passed, and then June and the first weeks of July. Nothing happened. On July 14th, 1970, exactly a year since my arrest, I went on strike. I refused to work. Despite the sympathetic treatment of Mr Alexander (Sandy) Angus, the Governor of Peterhead, the Scottish Home Department ordered that I should go into solitary confinement. Mr Angus, one of the many people convinced of my innocence, had no choice but to obey the order. Apart from the two months – when I co-operated with the prison authorities on the advice of my lawyers – I was to remain in solitary confinement until the day of my release six years later. It was to be the longest spell of solitary in a British prison since they ceased hanging hungry men for stealing sheep!

With a change of Government after the Tories won a general

election, Scotland got a new Secretary of State, Mr Gordon Campbell MP (now Lord Campbell of Croy). My backers – Mr Beltrami, Mr Fairbairn and my MP Mr McElhone – petitioned the new arrival for my release. Still nothing happened.

It was time to attack another flank.

Solitary confinement, as I have said too often already in this book, gives a man a lot of time – time to brood destructively or plan constructively, to think aimless thoughts or to study subjects of value. I had begun to study Scottish law. Waddell had already been jailed for lying at my trial. I was still anxious to prove that the police officers who had rigged the identification parade had also lied. I came across the ancient device of a Bill of Letters, a process which allows a private citizen to take criminal court action against other parties. I decided I would get a Bill of Letters against the police so that I could prosecute them for perjury.

My lawyers were not optimistic. They felt the court would lean towards the Crown Office – but I pressed ahead anyway. The major problem: a Bill of Letters can only be issued by the courts; in other words, you had to get the court's permission to go to court! I had no reason to be confident of the impartiality of the judiciary where I was involved. The complexity of my legal problem was not helped when I got shipped off to a special punishment unit at Porterfield prison, Inverness, where I was to spend four months in The Hole. My offence? I gave a released prisoner a pamphlet I had written about my case. I wanted him to take it to the Press. Instead, he got drunk, was arrested and was searched. My punishment? The Hole, a cage within a cell, a heavily barred area within a cell just big enough to take my 'bed'. Even this is a misnomer for it was no bed in the conventional sense – merely a wooden platform raised above the floor. There was no chair, no table. Not an ideal place to study the law.

My only satisfaction from this long and, thank God, almost forgotten period was my meeting with a screw known as Bully Boy. He had been moved from the prison pig farm to look after The Hole.

'Is it true that all the pigs wagged their tails the day you were promoted?' I asked.

'I dinna ken what ye mean,' he replied, mystified.

I smiled. My lawyers were worried about the effect of the constant solitary on my mental health. At least I had not deteriorated to such an extent as to be less intelligent than the staff. In the meantime I was visited by solicitors, Len Murray and Joe Beltrami, and agreed that they should jointly act on my behalf in order to ensure that the interests of justice would be furthered. This meeting took place in Peterhead prison.

The politicians were doing nothing. The law was doing nothing. Then, out of the blue, Ian Waddell did something quite spectacular. Early in 1973 – two and a half years after my arrest – he announced that he wanted to confess to the murder! Suddenly my case, which to all intents and purposes had been forgotten by the people of Scotland, was to come back into the news with a bang!

Waddell had served his sentence for the perjury, and then another eight months of a year's sentence for possessing a loaded revolver. In one of those coincidences lucky for me, he had been represented on the revolver charge by Mr Beltrami who, although he was no longer acting for me, still maintained a passionate interest in my case. Waddell's reason for wanting to confess, he said, was in gratitude to Mr Beltrami for 'getting him off' with such a light sentence. There was another reason, of course – money, a lot of it. He was prepared to confess to a newspaper or broadcasting network which would pay him £30,000 for his trouble. News of the prospective confession reached the ears of David Scott, one of the many Glasgow journalists who had done everything in their power to help my case. Scott, a BBC reporter, and producer Ken Vass, were waiting outside the gate of Barlinnie prison as Waddell shuffled to freedom on February 3rd, 1973. Scott was carrying a concealed tape recorder. Waddell was prepared to give every detail of what happened in the Rosses' house, he said, with the exception of one fact: he would not name his accomplice.

All five arranged a meeting at the office of Waddell's solicitor, Mr Robert Gibson, but he didn't arrive. Two days later Scott and Vass tracked him down again. The transcript of the tape recording they made is given in Ludovic Kennedy's book:

Scott So what are your plans now, Ian?

Waddell I want to get all this finished as soon as possible . . . I'll need to leave before I get assassinated. The police'll assassinate me first chance they get.

Vass See, we'll have problems persuading our colleagues what the outcome might be before we start talking to them on any other basis. Our people keep asking me, does this mean in fact that you will establish that Paddy Meehan is innocent or not?

Waddell Aye, I will establish that. It must be under the truth drug. That is the only way I can't be charged as far as I know.

Vass But you will certainly establish his innocence?

Waddell I'll establish that.

Waddell had presumably remembered my application to the High Court in 1969, asking to be questioned under the influence of a truth drug. Remembering that the court had refused me permission to take such a test, he must have assumed that any confession under the drug would not be called as evidence. The trio discussed details of the raid on the Ross home, and the tape goes on:

Scott What would be the greatest thing you could say that would sway people to believe that Meehan was innocent?

Waddell I done the murder!

Vass You actually tied them up, did you?

Waddell Uh-huh.

Scott You and this other fellow.

Waddell Aye . . . I still maintain she wasn't murdered . . . she wasn't murdered, know what I mean?

Scott Yes.

Waddell She wasn't intentionally murdered . . .

The final question of the interview set yet another mystery.

Scott You've said you'd have to leave town because you'd be assassinated. I mean, who would be after you in this case?

Waddell The police.

Scott Just the police? I mean, not your accomplice?

Waddell Aye probably him an' all.

Note that there was no suggestion that I would be after him, or rather any of my friends. Just the police – or his accomplice. Why should Waddell fear the police in such a dramatic way? Was it perhaps that he knew, as I knew, that the police had rigged my trial? And that they might want to cover their tracks? At last, I thought, the truth is coming out. Or was it?

Thirty thousand pounds is a great deal of money, and no newspaper could be found to fork out a small fortune for the rambling confession of a small time crook. In the end, Scott went ahead and prepared a programme. It went out in July, despite the legal objections from Waddell, who had suddenly realized the danger of his situation. With Waddell's confession, and the new evidence about the jiggery-pokery at the ID parade, my new solicitor, Mr Len Murray, prepared yet another petition to the Secretary of State asking for the Royal Prerogative of Mercy. For the first time for two years, I was confident once more. Yet in October 1973 Mr Campbell, the Secretary of State, announced that 'after discussions with the Lord Advocate, I have decided that there is no further action I can take.' As Ludovic Kennedy comments acidly in his book:

These continued refusals by the authorities to recognize that justice had miscarried were now occurring with monotonous regularity and are one of the case's most depressing features.

In my solitary cell, I went back to my law books to continue my struggle to win a Bill of Letters.

Outside, the sheer obstinacy of the Scottish authorities to admit their mistake rebounded against them. Instead of damping down interest in the case – which I presume was their intention – they sparked off massive press and television activity. The *Sunday Times* investigated the case, and in March 1974, MP Mr McElhone rose in the House of Commons to demand an impartial enquiry with a view to a Royal Pardon. Another General Election intervened, Labour won, and back to the Secretary of State's job came my old adversary, Willie Ross. He was to prove as stubborn as ever. In August 1974, five years after my arrest, he announced that after more careful and exhaustive consideration with – guess who? – the Lord Advocate, 'I have come to the conclusion that there are no grounds that would justify recommending the excercise of the Royal Prerogative of Mercy or taking any action in the case.'

The intransigence of the Secretary of State's office and the Lord Advocate were becoming a national scandal. As Kennedy wrote:

I thought this a shocking and perverse decision. It should have been clear to the authorities by now that the time for stone-walling was over, that there were, to put it at its lowest, the gravest doubts about Meehan's guilt, and the only way to resolve them and allay public unease was not by secret consultations which smacked of cover-up, but through an officially appointed independent enquiry whose findings would be made public.

The clause in that long sentence which attracted my eye was 'secret consultations which smacked of cover-up.' Cover-up of what? Were a cabinet minister and the Lord Advocate of Scotland prepared to fly in the teeth of outraged public opinion to protect the reputations of a handful of police officers? Or were there more sinister undercurrents on the move?

The sensations followed one upon the other. Mr Ross, who had lost his wife and the peace of deserved old age at the hands of two sadistic brutes, announced that he no longer believed that I had committed the murder. As if this weren't enough, Waddell was still going the rounds of Glasgow newspapers 'hawking' his confession. He made a detailed statement to Gordon Airs, chief reporter of the *Daily Record*, and his colleague Charles Beaton, and gave them seventeen facts about the Rosses' bungalow and the events of the attack. Airs and Beaton spent two weeks checking the points one by one against reports which had appeared in the newspapers. They came to the conclusion that Waddell was giving information which had never been publicly aired. In other words, Waddell could only have gone into so much detail if he had been at the house on the night of the raid. The *Daily Record* did not use the story. Instead, they sent the confession to the Lord Advocate who decided to take no action. Instead, he passed it on to the Secretary of State. Public figures were still dancing round the mulberry bush.

In September 1974, I finally went to court to apply for my Bill of Letters to take perjury proceedings against the three police officers. It was the same court in Edinburgh which had seen my conviction five years earlier. It was about as just! The judges rejected my application because, they said, this 'would open the floodgates to private prosecution which our system of criminal prosecution has been devised and developed to prevent.' Once again the interest of the law had been judged to override the interests of justice!

177

In June 1975, the Secretary of State asked to see a draft copy of Ludovic Kennedy's book. I hoped it might change Mr Ross's mind. But by this time, I was used to Stone Wall Willie. On October 10th, he announced he had once again consulted the Lord Advocate, and once again decided there were no grounds for a Royal Pardon. This enraged Kennedy as much as it enraged me. Kennedy wrote:

Why did the Secretary of State refuse an enquiry? As his decision was arrived at in secret, it is impossible to say. But it looks as though either – and I find this almost impossible to believe – because he still had not the slightest doubt about Meehan's guilt, or – and I am sorry to say it – he was fearful of what such an enquiry might reveal. What other explanation can there be?

What other explanation, indeed?

Still the pressure mounted. The Scottish National Party called for an enquiry into the case. The *Sunday Times*, a formidable campaigning newspaper, took up the cry. And Ian Waddell was still helping me along, not now for money – he seemed to be enjoying his notoriety. On October 14th, 1975, the *Scottish Daily News* carried another confession by Waddell on its front page. Surely, now, something must happen?

The papers were full of it, and the television people were soon on the trail. Waddell confessed before the BBC cameras and the remarkable interview was eventually shown on the Panorama programme. Then Joe Beltrami came forward with a bombshell. Mr Beltrami – how often his name crops up – was able to make his explosive revelation when Tank McGuinness was killed in a street brawl. McGuinness, Waddell's accomplice on the night of the murder, had been defended by Mr Beltrami in a later case. Under the cover of privilege that governs conversations between solicitor and client, McGuinness had admitted being the Second Man. The confession had placed Mr Beltrami in a terrible ethical quandary. It was a fearful weapon in the battle he was helping fight, but he was unable to use it because of ethical red-tape. On McGuinness's death, the widow gave the solicitor permission to tell the world the truth. Even the Secretary of State's office could not stand so much heat. Two senior police officers were asked to investigate the case. Mr Beltrami advised the Law Society of

Scotland of these climactic developments, and then gave the two senior officers a detailed account of his numerous meetings with McGuinness. And on the 22nd April 1976, a senior prison officer came to my cell at Peterhead and handed me a document to sign.

'I think you will be out on parole in a few weeks,' he said, 'so fill in the form.'

I exploded. 'Why the hell should I fill in any forms?' I demanded. 'I'm not taking any bloody parole. You can't parole a man for a crime he did not commit.' It was my final act of defiance.

On May 19th, yet another new Secretary of State for Scotland, Mr Bruce Millan, rose in the green-leathered chamber of the House of Commons to announce that vital new evidence had come forward in the Meehan case – the McGuinness confession.

'The new information which has become available since the death of McGuinness, taken along with the earlier considerations relevant to this case, has convinced me that it would be wrong for Patrick Meehan to remain in prison convicted of murder,' he told a hushed gathering of MPs. 'I have, therefore, decided to recommend the exercise of the Royal Prerogative to grant a Free Pardon. Mr Meehan is being released today . . .'

The document was headed by the Queen's flowing signature – ELIZABETH R. In beautifully convoluted jargon, it read:

ELIZABETH THE SECOND, by the Grace of God of the United Kingdom of Great Britain and Northern Ireland and of Our other Realms and Territories, QUEEN, Head of the Commonwealth, Defender of the Faith, to all to whom these Presents shall come;

GREETING!

WHEREAS Patrick Connolly Meehan was at the High Court holden at Edinburgh on the twenty-fourth day of October 1969 convicted of murder and sentenced to life imprisonment;

NOW KNOW YE that We in consideration of some circumstances humbly represented unto Us and of Our Prerogative Royal, Proper Motion, and Royal Clemency are graciously pleased to extend Our Grace and Mercy to the said Patrick Connolly Meehan and to grant him Our Free Pardon in respect of the said conviction thereby pardoning, remitting and releasing him all pains, penalties and punishments whatsoever that from the said conviction may come.

Given at Our Court at St James the 19th day of May 1976 in the
Twenty-fifth Year of Our Reign

BY HER MAJESTY'S COMMAND
(signed) Bruce Millan

I have to record that, rather than shouting in joy, I remarked:
'How can she pardon me for something I didn't do?'

It should have been the end but it was really the beginning of a
new set of problems. It was marvellous to be free again, to be
with Betty and the children and good friends, to go for a drive
and pop into a pub for a half of whisky. I had many friends to
thank, the lawyers, the pressmen, Ludovic Kennedy, who had
given such unflagging support. One 'thank you' cost me £4,000.
The Scottish *Daily Record* offered me £6,000 for my *exclusive*
story, which would have prevented me giving an interview to the
BBC's David Scott, whose efforts in my cause had been so
strenuous and so vital. I gave David his interview – and the
Record gave me £2,000 for the rest. Money was still to be a problem, of course, for I had decided one thing above all: I was going
straight!

If I had been less stubborn, perhaps I would have realized the
stupidity of a life of crime twenty years earlier. We all have our
lessons to learn from life: perhaps I am just a slow learner! The
authorities tried belatedly to put things right. They offered me
£7,000 compensation – £1,000 for each year, six of them in
solitary confinement! I would have received more on the dole for
those seven years, and still walked down the street a free man. I
rejected the offer.

They tried Ian Waddell for the murder and that, too, was another complete shambles. The only evidence against him was his
confessions – and they had not been made to the police or
officers of the court. He chose not to repeat them – which shows
that he does have some sense, for a repetition would have cost
him certain life imprisonment. And – strangely – there was no
damning forensic evidence against him. In the end, they found
him Not Guilty. The only debt to society for the death of
Rachel Ross had already been paid – by me. Wrongly. Even at
this late date, the Scottish judiciary was unwilling to admit that
it had made a grave error.

*

Waddell's trial was full of irony, judicial manoeuvring and – from the police side – glaring inconsistencies which were of deep interest to me. The irony came from the fact that Waddell's defence included an impeachment against me. They were to try to incriminate me for the murder, exactly the reverse of my own defence all those years before. So it was going to be a mirror-image trial – the sort of mirror Lewis Carroll made famous in *Alice through the Looking Glass*. The judicial manoeuvring started on day one, and lasted until the very end. The first argument was that Waddell could not be tried because I had already been convicted of the crime – and as there was no suggestion that Waddell and I had ever met until well after the murder, therefore, Waddell could not have committed it. So my conviction was being taken as evidence to clear Waddell. Yet I had a Queen's Pardon.

This set the legal wigs nodding and shaking. Was the Pardon an admission that I was Not Guilty – that my conviction had been quashed? Or was it merely that I had been 'pardoned' or 'forgiven' – and the conviction still stood? They never settled that one – and haven't till this day. I still don't know if I am a convicted murderer or not – despite the fact I never committed a murder, and everyone in the world seems to accept my innocence. So an innocent man can also be a convicted man! That's a pretty damnable cloud to leave hanging over a man's head.

The question of whether my conviction stood or not was not settled, but the court decided to go ahead with the case against Waddell. That meant I had to give evidence – and so did the police. And it was during the police evidence that the pitiful bungling in the investigations became known to an astonished public. For Tank McGuinness, after leaving the Ross bungalow, had actually been stopped on suspicion by two cruising policemen. He gave them a cock and bull story about getting drunk and missing his bus back to Glasgow. The policemen, Inspector Hepburn and Sgt McNeil, who at the time were junior officers, believed the story and *actually gave McGuiness a lift to the bus station*! When news of the murder broke, Hepburn and McNeil – no doubt cursing their own gullibility – made out a detailed report. This, they said in sworn evidence, they gave to the then Detective Sergeant Aitcheson. This testimony was to cause the prosecution a major embarrassment because when Aitcheson, now Detective Superintendent, took the stand, he denied that he had ever received the Hepburn and McNeil reports. Someone, somewhere, had a very poor memory!

The McGuinness incident proved, once and for all, that the police investigation had either been a matter of gross incompetence – or a deliberate plot to frame me. For McGuiness was a known criminal whose previous record had involved incidents of entering houses *and tying up the occupants*! Even the most uninformed member of the general public surely knows – from crime series on television if nothing else – that the first step of any detective investigating a serious crime is to study the MO – the *modus operandi*. Some criminals fall into such a routine on jobs that their MO can be as unmistakable as their fingerprints. A check of Scottish criminal records would have produced McGuiness's name within minutes as a man with a predilection for 'tying up' capers, always a risky tactic as Mrs Ross's death so grimly proved. And here were two police officers who had given a lift to a suspicious man in the right place at the right time.

Were Hepburn and McNeil ever shown a photograph of McGuinness and asked: 'Is this the man you took to the bus station?' The answer to that is an incredible – and to me, unacceptable – No! Yet at the time the two officers were making out their reports, Chief Superintendent Struthers was making frantic appeals for assistance to any member of the general public who might have seen any suspicious people near the Rosses' home on the night of the raid. If there were ever any doubts in my mind that some police officers were determined to nail me, rather than unmask the genuine culprits, this evidence was the final, total and utter clincher.

When I was called into the witness box, I shocked the court into an amazed silence by insisting that I had been framed – and that I had been framed on the orders of British Intelligence. The media went wild. The *Daily Express* reported the story on November 25th, 1976 under the headline splashed across eight columns: *MEEHAN: SPY CHIEFS SET ME UP*. In the subheadline, I was quoted: *BRITISH INTELLIGENCE USED ME TO SPRING GEORGE BLAKE FROM JAIL. THEN I WAS*

182

FRAMED. In the story beneath the headline, the *Express* reported that Waddell's QC, Mr James Law, had asked me why British Intelligence should want to frame me. I had replied:

'Because I knew too much. I was framed to put me out of circulation as I was about to go to Germany.'

The report of the exchange continued:

Mr Meehan, asked if Intelligence was afraid he would release information he had to the Russians, replied: 'They knew I was going to Germany. They were afraid that I would end up behind the Curtain – where I would be interrogated.'
Mr Law 'In other words, the information you had was of value to the Russians?'
Mr Meehan 'I would say so.'
Mr Law 'It was in order to prevent you getting that information to the Russians that you were framed and put in prison for life?'
Mr Meehan 'I think they were going to put me out of the way until such time as they thought it was safe.'

Whether the court believed me or not, I do not know. It did not believe the case against Waddell, for – as I have already said – he was found Not Guilty and walked away a free man. If there had not been sensation enough, there was one last bombshell to come from, of all people, the judge, Lord Robertson. He chose his summing up as the time to publicly lambast the Secretary of State for Scotland for recommending my Queen's Pardon. Puffing away angrily at this intervention by the politicians into the running of the courts, he declared: 'If the Executive are going to interfere in such a way in the administration of justice, there is no end to it. One of the great bulwarks of liberty in this country is threatened.'

I stormed out of court, telling reporters who besieged me that I was going to tear up my Queen's Pardon – after seven years of effort, it was not worth the paper it was written on. The Judiciary, it would appear, wanted to have the last word. In some strange way, my case had threatened 'one of the great bulwarks of liberty'. What about my liberty? The Scottish judiciary may well be proud of their independence from the politicians, but can they be proud of the treatment they meted out to me?

*

As I write this, I am still waiting to give evidence before what, I hope, will be the final enquiry into the Ross murder and my wrongful conviction. I have before me an invitation to appear before Lord Hunter, whom the Government appointed to carry out an investigation into the affair. I hope – I pray – that this may eventually lead to the truth. I hope, too, that the ghost of Mrs Rachel Ross may at last know some peace. But I have to admit that I am doubtful that the full truth behind the Meehan Affair will ever be made public – at least, not during my lifetime. I have no doubts whatsoever that I was framed for the murder. The unanswered question is: which hands pulled the strings to make a democratic country match the tyranny of the dictatorships? It would be comfortable for most Britons, I am sure, to think that I was merely the victim of a few warped police officers, determined to get a conviction at all costs. It has happened before – and it will happen again. But in all my vast experience of police methods, I have never once believed that senior police officers would build an elaborate frame-up on a murder charge without orders from the very top. The risks of putting forward concocted evidence into the blinding glare of publicity that surrounded the Ross murder were far too great to be born from the simplistic idea that convictions mean promotions in the police world. If this is so, who then, decided upon such a risky course?

I have already gone at great length into my chain of suspicion which led to my ill-fated sojourn behind the iron curtain. The mysterious Hector, the treacherous Sheila, my treatment at Nottingham jail – a known escapee suddenly switched from top security prisoner to red-band trusty, to the total bewilderment of the staff. Some of the world's leading authorities believe that George Blake's escape was engineered by British Intelligence for motives which, even after all these years, remain totally obscure. It is a belief which, according to many books on the subject, is shared by the CIA and by the French and West German secret services. But my chain of suspicion did not end with the Blake escape and my release from prison on the Isle of Wight. Who was the German dollybird? Was my telephone tapped? Why was the Special Branch following me? Who were the young man and his colleague in the van keeping watch on Betty's flat?

When I had been sentenced for the Ross murder, I demanded the return of the address book which had been seized in the search of the flat – the address book which had contained Griffiths' phone number. It had also contained another piece of information which apparently absorbed the 'authorities' – whoever they were. I had written the number of the mysterious van in that book. When, after numerous protests, the book was finally returned to me in Peterhead prison, two pages had been torn out. One carried the note of Griffiths' phone number. The other bore the registration number of the mysterious van! I was requested to sign a form acknowledging the return of the book. Before doing so I examined the book in the presence of a senior officer, Mr Davidson.

'Will you please initial that two pages have been torn out,' I asked him. My request puzzled him, but he did put his signature to verify that the pages were missing. I needed him as a witness that the book had been tampered with. More mysterious scraps of paper!

Why had the police – and the Special Branch, to boot – kept such a careful watch on me after my release? Were they hoping that they might trap me in the commission of another crime? If so, they must have been terribly disappointed, for I kept a 'clean sheet' – even my trip to Stranraer had been undertaken with the greatest reluctance. As I had committed no crime which – in a democratic society – was the only possible reason for throwing me into jail, did someone somewhere, decide that I must be framed? It does, I admit, seem far-fetched. But so, too, do many of the exploits of the spies who were the talk of Britain in the 1960s.

If Blake were sent back to Russia to spread 'disinformation' – deliberately confusing data – it was essential that the Russians should think his escape genuine. If you can accept this hypothesis, take your mind one step further to the elegant office of the head of the British Secret Service. Plans to throw a massive spanner into the works of the KGB are going splendidly – until one day, a crooked nobody from the Glasgow slums has the temerity to write to Chapman Pincher saying that he warned the authorities of Blake's likely escape. I doubt the Secret Service likes conducting its business on the front page of the *Daily Express*. If I were 'M' – or whatever they call their super-spy – I would say: 'This man has got to be silenced.' Wouldn't you? Will we ever know the full truth? I don't know – but there are many people who believe what I believe.

A group of prisoners in Peterhead jail wrote a folk song, which was smuggled out and performed by the late Matt McGinn, one of Scotland's best-known entertainers. My sixteen-year-old son took the liberty of rewriting the song to make it more factual:

The Ballad of Paddy Meehan

I'll tell ye aw a story
If ye'll no tell anyone
'Cause the British Secret Service
Wid like to keep it mum

Ye've heard o Paddy Meehan
The Glasgow peterman
Who visits aw the bonny banks
At midnight – if he can

Well Paddy wis up in Peterhead
A rotting down The Hole
Sure it must have been bloody awful
Tae be living like a mole

They framed the man for murder
An' threw him in the can
But Paddy wisnae guilty
Cause he's no a violent man

Noo ah know the story
An ah know the tale
Why the British Secret Service
Locked Paddy up in jail

Dae ye remember years ago
'Twas nineteen sixty three
When Paddy took a powder
An went to Germany

Behind the Berlin Wall he went
A convict on the run
He didnae go for freedom
And he didnae go for fun

Well the British Secret Service
Helped Paddy on the way
For Paddy was a puppet
In a game they had to play

When the Commies tried to brainwash
They got an awful fright
For inside Paddy's head they found
A stick of gelignite

Well Paddy told his story
('Cause Paddy's full o' tricks)
An whit dae ye know a spy was sprung
In nineteen sixty six

So Paddy knew a thing or two
He figured this an' that
And the British Secret Service knew
That Paddy smell't a rat

Then Paddy came to realize
That he'd been used as bait
The British Secret Service
Jist done a Watergate

There's an awful lot of lawyers
Who'll tell ye whit they think
That the case of Paddy Meehan
Is gonny cause a stink

The British Secret Service
Have done poor Paddy wrong
If they hadn't framed him down in Ayr
They'd have made him Bible John

That's no aw the story
There's much more ah kin tell
But ahm no gonny risk it
Cause they might frame me as well

I like the last stanza the best. 'That's not all the story, there's
much more I can tell . . .' I believe that many of us in this world
are destined to be puppets – manipulated by unseen hands to per-
form little understood acts for reasons shrouded in mystery.
George Blake, Gordon Lonsdale, the Krogers – they were
puppets, dancing for unseen masters. I think Paddy Connolly
Meehan was a puppet too. Until someone decided to cut the
string.

Brian Moynahan
Airport International 80p

The sensational book that takes the lid off the world of international air travel. How smugglers operate and how they're caught . . . when and how luggage is pilfered . . . how air traffic control really works . . . how airports cope with a crash landing . . . which are the dangerous airports that pilots try to avoid . . . your chances of survival in an air crash.

Based on extensive research by Brian Moynahan of the *Sunday Times Insight* team.

John Slater
Just Off The Motorway £1.75

Here's the handbook you've been waiting for. *Just Off The Motorway* traces all the facilities available when you turn off at every junction on every one of Britains ten major motorways. Detailed research, careful sampling and more than 150 maps show you where you can find any service you need . . . eating, drinking, overnight stops, 24-hour breakdown services, petrol . . . cheaper and better by turning off at a junction and driving for no more than three miles off the motorway.

Magnus Pyke
Butter Side Up! 75p

Could we soon be eating dormice for dinner? Does bread really fall more often butter side up . . . or butter side down? Britain's most popular scientist asks some not-so-silly questions and comes up with some very sensible answers.

'. . . achieves the small miracle of evoking in print Dr Pyke's now familiar torrent of talk' SUNDAY TELEGRAPH

John Nicholson
Habits 75p

'Each chapter deals with something most of us do, consciously or unconsciously, every day – living with other people and our surroundings, eating, remembering, winning and losing, believing, walking, smoking, pretending . . . jargon is kept to a minimum . . . the book is elegant and restrained' SPECTATOR

David Taylor
Zoovet 75p

The drowning hippopotamus and the arthritic giraffe . . . The
pornographic parrot and the motorcycling chimp . . . Just a few of the
patients that are all in a day's work for David Taylor, one of the
world's most unusual vets. *Zoovet* is his story of the hilarity and the
heartache of animal-doctoring by jetliner across the globe.

'Good humour and abounding energy on every page'
WASHINGTON POST

Richard Walker
Stillwater Angling 95p

When this book first appeared an unbelievable twenty-five years ago
it was acclaimed as years ahead of its time, a revolutionary approach to
fishing for carp, perch, tench, chub, pike and rudd and the best guide
to hooking the really big ones.

'The best on its subject' THE FIELD

Brian Clarke
The Pursuit of Stillwater Trout £1.00
Illustrated, with a foreword by Hugh Falkus

'Apart from being a top-class book on nymph fishing and stillwater
trouting in general, it is above all a great book just to read'
ANGLING TIMES

John Gooders
Where To Watch Birds in Europe £1.75

This indispensable guide to the bird life of Europe covers twenty-seven
countries, with details of what birds to look for and where to find them,
their routes, access, permits, local societies, and seasonal variations in
bird populations.

'The fruit of an immense amount of research' SUNDAY TELEGRAPH

Brian John
Pembrokeshire £1.25

Illustrated

'History, topography, industry, architecture, geography, industrial archaeology – a wide-ranging study of this unique region . . . a world of fascination and new knowledge' WESTERN TELEGRAPH

'Brian John's expertise shows through on every page' WEST WALES GUARDIAN

Clive Carter
Cornish Shipwrecks – the North Coast £1.25

Illustrated. Between 1800 and 1920 – excluding heavy wartime losses – more than a thousand vessels were wrecked along the north coast of Cornwall. Here are unforgettable pages of Cornish maritime history and the men who made it – lifeboatmen, coastguards, excisemen and the notorious 'wreckers' . . .

Colm O Lochlainn
Irish Street Ballads 90p

A choice collection of over one hundred of the finest songs that Erin ever sang. From 'The Flower of Magherally' to 'The Star of Donegal' – here are songs for the rebel and the ranter, the traveller, tinker and tailor – for all the world and Garrett Reilly!

More Irish Street Ballads 90p

A second and every bit as splendid collection of ballads, collected and annotated by Colm O Lochlainn.

B. H. Liddell Hart
The Other Side of the Hill £1.25

The classic account of Germany's generals, their rise and fall . . . Here
is the Second World War as it was seen by the men who commanded
the Panzer Divisions and the might of the Wermacht – a unique
account in the annals of human conflict.

'The most formidable military writer of the age' A. J. P. TAYLOR

'Fascinating and even sensational' ROBERT HENRIQUES

Gerold Frank
The Boston Strangler 80p

The most bizarre series of murders since Jack the Ripper; the greatest
man-hunt in the annals of modern crime; Albert DeSalvo, brutal
sexual psychopath, who murdered thirteen women and held a city in
the icy grip of terror for eighteen hideous months.

'Tells us everything about the case . . . chronologically, as it happened
. . . the result is completely satisfying' NEW YORKER

Martin Gosch and Richard Hammer
The Luciano Testament 95p

America's most notorious gangster tells all . . . Bribe by bribe, killing
by killing, Charlie 'Lucky' Luciano came to be *capo di tutti capi*, boss of
all the bosses, from Capone to Dutch Schulz and Bugsy Siegel.
Companion to society women, confidant of politicians, he bought
judges, union leaders, policemen to change the face of the Mafia. Told
against the violent backcloth of America's underworld from the
twenties to the fifties, this is the controversial story of his rise and fall.